Venna H:

Story of an Eastern Mormon Convert

Julia Farr

Alpha Editions

This edition published in 2024

ISBN : 9789362921130

Design and Setting By
Alpha Editions
www.alphaedis.com
Email - info@alphaedis.com

Contents

PREFACE.

First in my thought as I wrote this little book were the young people in the West, who enjoy the blessings of their religion, without realization of the persecution of their missionaries on the fighting line. Perhaps if they read my description of religious conditions in the East, they will more highly prize the truths they possess, and strive to live more worthily, that their lives may contribute to the spread of the Restored Gospel.

George Eliot has said we cannot even *think* a good thought but that we become a power against evil. So it behooves every Latter-day Saint to live up to the *very best* that he or she may be a power in this great work of God's.

Second in my thought were the people of the East—those with whom I have lived and worked since my birth in Brooklyn, N. Y. I wish to say to them, I hope no one of my friends will think that they are depicted in the characters of my novel.

I am aware that I have offered no convincing arguments concerning the "Mormon" faith. But I hope that some of my readers may feel a distinction between the religious natures of my characters, and consequently be led to investigate the truths of "Mormonism" for themselves.

My experience has been that one who desires the truth can always find it, but never within the two covers of a short work of fiction. Therefore my object has been simply to endeavor to awaken a *desire* for truth, which may lead the reader into deeper researches.

I know that no great literary ability is shown in this little volume of mine, but I dare to put it before the world and ask every one to read it—why?— Because I have God's assurance that the weakest effort of man can do much good, if that effort is put forth for the upbuilding of His Kingdom upon earth.

—

CHAPTER I.

There is that in youth, untarnished by the world's experience, that invites the whisperings of diviner things.

"Very fine! Very fine!" exclaimed Professor Strausbey as the last note of the girl's violin died away in its tender pianissimo.

Little Venna drew a long breath of satisfaction, shook her curls as if freeing herself from some unseen power and looked up smiling.

"I almost lost my breath," she said, smiling. "Do you know, Professor, when I play that wonderful music, I can scarcely breathe, and it feels as though some one was holding my hand for me and making my bow move!"

The Professor laughed his answer. "Genius gripping your hand, my dear!" Then seriously, "Don't you think you could do just one more hour's practice a day? You know I'm expecting very big things of you at April's concert. Only one month more!"

"Oh, yes, indeed I can! And I'll surprise even you at that concert! I'll have everyone bowing low to my genius!" she added, her brown eyes fairly dancing with the eagerness of ambition.

"Maybe! You won't, if you slide over your lessons as shamefully as this one," he returned in a suddenly changed tone. "That last was the only good one today."

To himself he was reiterating "Genius! Genius!" but he seldom praised without regretting the fact and immediately serving the antidote to his overconfident pupil. He was quite sure flattery was poison.

To herself, Venna's fourteen wise years were as constant testimony that she knew all things, lived all things, and would finally conquer all things.

One of her relatives who criticized her self-confidence, wrote in her album,

> "When ambitious youth, secure and proud,
> Ascends the ladder, leaning on a cloud!
> O then, Venna, beware!"

Venna immediately wrote under it,

> "Better to ascend and have a fall
> Than to sit down and never climb at all.
> If I fall, I'll climb still higher.
> But wait until the cloud is drier!"

There was no doubt about Venna's brilliancy—the family and all her friends agreed upon that. But her self-confidence—it was almost appalling. She was so bewitchingly lovable that no one called it conceit, but—well, we will not analyze her character too closely at this early period. She was a bundle of possibilities, presumably exceptional.

Venna took the Professor's rebuke with pretended sobriety.

"Of course, I'll try to do better. You know I hate monotony and dislike practicing the same thing over and over again. I'd much rather play just what I feel like." Then suddenly beaming with assurance, she smilingly declared, "I'm sure I'd do wonders if you would let me show you how I wish to be taught. Just let me take up theme after theme, just as I wish to, and develop naturally. I should follow nature! 'Consider the lily, how it grows'"—

"Enough, young lady!" interrupted her Professor with dutiful sternness. "You'll do as I wish, if I'm to teach you. Of course, you are too young (here Venna's curls gave a pronounced shake) to appreciate anything scientific yet, but nevertheless you must accept what I tell you. Music is science as well as poetry, and the science of it, I am here to teach."

"Oh, yes, I suppose I must imbibe it all," the girl answered dubiously. "But science! How I hate the word. It reminds me of all kinds of animals and creeping things being cut up on our laboratory table at school—just before lunch hour at that. Professor! Just think of it! But poetry! O how I love it! But let me play one more etude to please you. Which one shall I dissect? They all belong to the same species of black beetle crawling up and down the eternal scale!"

"Venna, shame on you!" came with a soft drawl, the tone of which seemed to say, "Venna, I'm charmed with you!"

The girl turned to see her aunt's round, mild face peering through the portieres.

"O auntie, have you been in the recess all the time? Why didn't you tell me and I would have said just the right thing!"

Here Professor Strausbey struck a vehement introductory chord which Venna understood to mean the finale of patience.

Taking her violin, she began her etude with slow, deliberate carefulness.

The lesson over, Venna helped her Professor into his coat, re-assuring him at the same time, "My next lesson will be perfect."

"I've heard that before," he laconically returned, taking his hat and half smiling into the bright upturned face with its large brown eyes and inquisitive, tilted nose. Bright brown curls artistically framed this picture of life, temperament and joyousness. So he thought, but he said tersely, "Plan less and do more!"

As the door closed upon him, Venna pulled aside the portieres.

"Auntie, isn't he the dear old *bear*?"

"He's right, dear," returned her aunt, pausing in her knitting. "You are too 'bubbly.' You must learn to concentrate more. But I suppose you are young"—

"Young! Oh, how I dislike that word! I get it every turn I make. Young! Just because I'm not tall like other girls! Indeed, I'm not too young for anything, auntie. Do you realize I'm four-tee-e-n?"

"Just think of it!" her aunt replied, laughing, as she drew Venna down beside her and stroked the rebellious curls. "Fourteen! Do you know what Longfellow says? 'Standing with reluctant feet, where the brook and river meet.'"

"But my feet are not reluctant," Venna replied gaily. "I can hardly keep them from running down the bank and jumping in. I long to set sail, auntie!"

"So did your mother, dearie," came the answer, suddenly serious. "Sail carefully, Venna, there are many hidden rocks."

Venna's bright face sobered and her energetic little figure relaxed as she kneeled down beside her aunt.

"Poor, dear mother! How I wish I could have known her and kissed away all her tears!"

For a moment, both were silent, thinking of the mother who died leaving a tiny baby to its lonely father and a faithful aunt. Venna had often heard the story.

The mother had loved a man unworthy of her affections. Her parents had begged the impulsive girl not to marry him. But she coaxed her own way, and after years of unhappiness, she was left a widow, broken in health and spirit. It was at this period of her mother's life, that Venna's father found, loved, and married her. For one year she knew the great love of a good man, and blossomed back into youth and joyousness, only to leave the world at the birth of her first child, Venna.

"Auntie, don't you think mother sometimes sees us here and knows how happy we are?"

As she asked the question, her eyes searched eagerly those of her aunt.

"That we don't know, dearie. Maybe. Some churches teach that our departed loved ones are in Paradise. Others say they sleep in their graves until the great resurrection day."

Venna gave a slight shiver. "I couldn't believe that. It sounds so awful to me."

"Why awful?" asked her aunt mildly. "If God has made it so, it must be all right."

"But, auntie, God loves us, and wouldn't let us stay in a cold, worm-eaten grave!" Again she shivered.

"If you didn't know it, what matter?" returned her aunt with a satisfied vagueness. "I wish you wouldn't take all those mysteries so to heart. Venna. It doesn't matter really, dear; you can believe the other way, if you wish."

"*Can* believe? How can I when no one tells me surely. Yes, I think I can," she added musingly. "It's like when I play my violin. There's some power I don't see brings music right into my soul. I feel it, but I can't explain. That same power makes me feel mother isn't in the grave. No, I'm sure she is often with us and knows how happy we are," she ended with confidence.

"Well, dearie, it's a good, happy thought and so keep it. You think so much about religion, Venna; don't you think you are old enough to join the Church?"

"Mercy, No!" was the laughing answer. "I wouldn't really know what to join. All my beloved aunties belong to different churches, and while I love you best, dear, how could I decide which was right. Besides, if I can be as good as Daddy, I'll be satisfied. He wouldn't join any one of them, and who can surpass him?"

"Your father is a great exception. However, he is a good Christian man, Venna; that is the secret of his life."

"Of course it is," replied the girl confidently. "And I want to be a Christian, too—just like him and like you, too, auntie," she added tactfully.

That night Venna was not home to dinner, so John Hastings and his sister sat alone in the cosy dining-room.

John Hastings was a rich man, and his home was one of the best on Fifth Avenue, New York. However, both he and his sister loved simplicity, and their city house as well as their country villa had no excess luxury, and spelled "Home" in every detail.

As they sat at this evening meal, the bright burning logs of the open fire-place lit up his strong, handsome features.

He smiled into the gentle, blue eyes of his sister.

"John," she said thoughtfully, "our little girl will be fourteen soon."

"Is it possible, Emily? My baby fourteen! Well, we must invite every mother's boy and girl we know and give her a dandy party!"

"Yes, of course, we'll do that. She's planning it already. But that's not what I'm thinking about."

"No? What then?" His keen, gray eyes looked surprised.

"It's just this, John. I've been thinking a great deal today about Venna's joining the Church. You know she's going to be a decided belle—her beauty, talent"—

"Naturally!" he interrupted gaily. "Why not, Emily?"

"Now don't you think she ought to enter life with some religious thought? Ought she not to join the Church, John?"

"Is she getting tired of her Sunday-school?" he asked, suddenly serious.

"Yes, I think she is. She says she's getting too big for it."

"Then why doesn't she teach? That would keep her in touch," he said with practical emphasis.

"That is just what I asked her and she replied, 'Dear me, auntie! If I had some youngsters under my wing, I'd teach them all the things I'd *like* to believe. Dr. Hansom would soon put me out!'"

John Hastings gave a delighted laugh.

"She could teach the Church all right, Emily!"

His sister crimsoned without answering.

"There, Emily! I know you love the Church and it's right and womanly you should. I didn't mean to hurt you. Yes, let Venna join. Of course she should. It will give her something to think of besides the frivolities. Every woman should have a ballast in her life. I'll tell her I certainly wish her to join the Church, Emily!"

"But she won't, John."

"Won't? Why not?"

"Because you're her ideal and you don't join. You are her stumbling block," she added more courageously.

Her brother looked thoughtfully into the fire.

"I am her ideal? Some joke! I'm no better than the next one!"

"In her eyes, you are, dear. I don't like to criticize you, John, but you have managed Dr. Hansom's business affairs of the Church for years, sat every

Sunday in your pew, and yet haven't joined the Church. Don't you think it's about time you did?"

"No and yes, Emily! I think I prefer staying out of it. I'm paid for my services. That's simply business. I've often told you the Church to me is a fine religious organization—nothing more. I help it along, don't I? I'm no more a Congregationalist than I am Methodist, Presbyterian or any other Church follower."

"Yes, John, but Dr. Hansom is so broad. You can believe almost anything and yet be admitted to his Church."

Her brother laughed.

"Now you've hit it just right. And the churches that are not *so broad* are *so narrow* that you get completely cramped inside their portals!"

"But, John, if it would influence Venna to join, wouldn't you sacrifice your preference?"

"Well, I guess that is one point worth considering. Our girl should have some religious influence, that is sure. We won't always be with her. And to join the Church practically means no difference to me. Just add my name to the many other Dr. Hansom worshippers!"

Emily's mild face lit up with gentle enthusiasm.

"Then I can tell Venna you've decided to join?"

"Why, yes, if you wish it."

Emily met his half-amused, tolerant gaze, with affectionate adoration.

"John," she said, simply, "you always do the best thing when it's necessary."

So Venna and her father joined Dr. Hansom's Congregational Church. John Hastings' act was for his daughter's sake, and Venna's easy compliance resulted from her adoration of "Daddy."

———

Four years passed over the Hastings home. Scientists tell us our characters either progress or retrograde. If this be so, the progressing and retrograding must have struck an equilibrium in the last four years of John Hastings' life and that of his sister. He was the same cool, practical man of affairs, without a single gray hair added above his high intellectual brow. Emily was the same mild, adoring sister and aunt. Perhaps both had acquired a still deeper pride and affection for Venna,—if that could be called a change.

And Venna? Watch her enter the library where her father sat, book in hand in his customary arm-chair by the fire place.

She was a few inches taller and somewhat slimmer and more graceful. Curls still rebelliously clustered around the same bright but more thoughtful countenance. Her general bearing was more pronounced in its dignified calling of supporting the accumulated knowledge of the last four years.

"Daddy, it's wonderful!" she exclaimed, as she approached and slid down upon the cushion beside him. "We have made so many plans today, I can scarcely realize what a wonderful Daddy and Auntie you are!" she continued, taking her father's hand and cuddling it affectionately against her cheek.

With his free hand, Hastings stroked her curls.

"So my petty thinks her debut affair will be a success?"

"Oh, wonderful! Auntie is planning every detail, regardless of expense. Flowers, music, supper—all to be perfect! Everyone I like in the whole wide world is coming. Just think of it!"

"Just as I wish it to be, dearie. Strange how a little bundle like you can be one big man's whole ambition!"

Venna met his gaze lovingly.

"O Daddy! Why is it? I really don't deserve it all."

"Yes, Venna, you deserve all I can give you. Do you know you are so like your mother now, that when I make you happy it seems as though I am doing it for her also."

"Daddy, you are." Her countenance became pensively thoughtful as she searched her father's face earnestly.

"What fancy now?" he asked tenderly, used to her sudden change of mood.

"No fancy, Daddy, real truth. Do you know mother is with me very often? Maybe that is why I grow so like her?"

"You've said that before, Venna. Just what have you in mind?"

Venna contemplated the fantastic logs as she tried to answer.

"I don't see mother, Daddy, but I feel her presence—Oh! so surely! My thoughts are as illusive as those flames. First here, then there. I can't seem to get any clear understanding of it, yet I know it is true. Don't you believe that she could be near us? Dr. Hansom says there may be guardian angels for all of us."

"Do you think, girlie, it's wise to think too much about the may-bes? Your imagination is very strong, Venna. I really wish you were more practical, not so much of a dreamer, dear."

"Then you wouldn't have such a wonderful musician in your family," she returned, smiling.

"Very true. I guess I don't want you changed after all. You're just like your mother and I've never found her equal elsewhere."

Venna pressed her father's hand in sympathy, and there were a few moments of thoughtful silence.

Hastings noticed a wistful sadness come to the brown eyes—a look which always bothered him.

"Why so pensive?" he asked gently.

Venna gave a little sigh.

"Lately, I've been thinking quite a lot about the 'may-bes' in religion. I've been talking to Dr. Hansom a great deal and he's so full of 'may-bes.' So are you. Daddy dear."

"So is the whole Christian world, honey. You know the Bible tells us that we see through a darkened glass. But 'enough to know is given'" he added with practical satisfaction.

"That may be. 'Enough to know is given,' but do we ponder enough over what is given? We seem so unsure of almost everything. There's a girl in my class at school who is a Christian Scientist. She claims she understands everything, but when I ask her questions, her answers are so hazy and confused."

"Why puzzle over those things, dear? You're too young to bother your head this way. What this world needs is good, wholesome manhood and womanhood. Not a lot of dreamers, filled with catch-penny ideas. Be your own bright self and live your young life naturally. Don't we give you everything, dear, to make you the happiest girl in New York? If there's anything lacking, say the word," he added, patting her curls.

"Oh, you're wonderful. Daddy!" she replied, smiling brightly at him. "I'm never really unhappy. I just love to sometimes sit alone and dream." Then softly she added, "It is only then that I feel mother is near me."

Hastings' keen eyes scanned her face anxiously.

"I guess you had a hard last year at school. I'm glad you've graduated for good, and decided not to go to college. Just think of your music now, plenty of fresh air and lots of fun! It doesn't do for girls to get weak nerves!"

"Weak nerves! How funny! I'm strong as strong can be!" she said, laughing joyously.

Hastings shook his head.

"Moods show overstrain. Come, get your hat. We'll take a brisk walk and drop in at a show tonight."

Venna jumped up delighted. She would rather go out with Daddy than do anything else in the world.

In a few minutes they were in the brisk November air, John Hastings adjusting his usual quick pace to the shorter, slower step of his daughter.

With all her bright energy, Venna's walking seemed a contradiction. It was rather slow, very deliberate, and with a dignified bearing that was very attractive.

In the street, nothing ever escaped her notice. She would always prefer to walk rather than ride. She hated her limousine. Cosmopolitan New York was a constant delight, and a walk down Broadway a pleasurable habit.

The brilliant lights, the gay theatre throng, the queer, oddly contrasted styles of dress affected by the girls with the powdered noses—all these were never-failing amusements. But deeper than this light attraction was the real human throb of the great city's throng, hurrying to and fro, some laughing, some anxious, some with a self-important strut of achieved success, others with the dogged defiance of failure and chagrin.

"The Great White Way! Was there ever anything so interesting?" thought Venna, appreciating with her bright mind the appealing contrasts. As yet she was too young to be saddened by the undercurrent of human longing and unrest.

Suddenly Venna exclaimed, "Listen, Daddy! There's a bunch singing hymns on the next corner. How great that sounds!"

In strong contrast to the surroundings, the solemn chorus of mixed voices were filling the air with "Nearer, my God, to Thee."

"How strange," thought Venna, "God doesn't seem here at all."

"Some street missionaries," Hastings replied seriously. "They certainly get the crowd. They aren't paid for it either." ("like the ministers in the Churches," he added to himself mentally.)

As they neared the little group of workers a very young girl with a violin stepped forward and started to play. She looked upon the small crowd gathered. Her hand trembled. She stopped short with embarrassment.

"O Daddy, see! She's so nervous. She's tried and can't go on!"

The crowd smiled. Some laughed. Before Hastings realized what his daughter had done, Venna stepped forward to the girl's side.

"Won't you let me play?" she asked softly.

Surprised and glad, the girl handed Venna her violin.

Then Hastings saw what seemed to him one of the unrealities Venna had talked of. Was it a dream or the impossible truth? There she stood, his darling, her genius making the violin fairly plead with the mixed crowd.

Suddenly she turned to the group of young workers.

"Sing!" she commanded as she struck a few chords of "Jesus, Lover of my Soul."

In two minutes the air was filled with the beautiful melody. The whole crowd joined and Venna stood leading them with a look on her young face that her father had never before seen.

He certainly didn't approve of this publicity, but something held him back until the last note was sung. Then he hastily stepped forward, "Come, dear, don't delay longer," he said with a gentle firmness which Venna knew meant a command.

With a happy smile she handed back the violin.

One of the young men, tall, manly, with gray eyes of shining enthusiasm, stepped to her side.

"We can't thank you enough. You have certainly drawn the crowd for us. Now I can preach."

She looked up into the earnest face.

"I would love to stay to hear you. May I, Daddy?"

"Not this time, Venna. Come, we will be late."

Hastings spoke brusquely. The spell was broken and he felt annoyed at the crowd gazing so intently at Venna.

The young preacher compelled her gaze.

"No time for the gospel message? Read these, then," he added, smiling into her eyes, as he handed her a few tracts.

Venna took them with a "Thank you," and as she walked away with her father, she heard the young preacher's first words ring out to the crowd.

"My friends, that Divine music has thrilled your souls. What prompted that young lady to stop? It was the Spirit of God, working in this city of worldliness and"—

Venna heard no more—her father was walking her rapidly away. She folded the tracts, and put them in her bag.

"You're not angry with me, Daddy?" she asked at last, breaking the silence as they swung down Broadway.

"Angry, child? No! But don't do it again. Your aunt would never approve of such unconventionalism. You are too impulsive. Be dignified—even in religion."

"But Christ went into the highways. Oh, I like that young preacher so! He didn't look as though he had any 'may-bes!'"

"Forget him, Venna. Now what theatre shall we go to?"

Venna decided and they were soon sitting comfortably in their box, listening to the newest light opera New York had to offer.

But for the first time, the girl was out of tune with her surroundings. She kept hearing the young preacher's penetrating voice.

"My friends, what prompted that young lady to stop? It was the Spirit of God, working in this great city of worldliness."

"Was that true?" she asked herself. "What prompted me to stop?" She couldn't tell. She just wanted to. But how novel an experience! She liked it. She would like to know that preacher. He was different to her gentlemen friends. Novelty always appealed to Venna. Well, she couldn't know him. So it was no use thinking about it, she wisely decided.

But on kneeling down to say her prayers before retiring that night, she added simply,

"Dear Father in heaven, help the young street preacher in his wonderful mission work for Thee."

The next morning Venna slept late. She awoke with a confused idea that her dream was truly real, in which she saw a great throng of people in front of her home, she herself standing at the door-way, begging them to come no farther.

She knew they were coming in search of the young street preacher, and that he was hiding in her house somewhere.

But the crowd was pressing forward. In vain she remonstrated with them. Forcibly closing the door, she locked it securely. Then she turned with bated breath, to see the young missionary by her side, hat in hand, smiling down at her composedly.

"You are safe!" she exclaimed excitedly.

"Thank you. But do not fear for me. God takes care of His own. However, I will never forget this kindness. It is the Spirit of God in your heart."

With these words he turned the key and reopened the door. At his appearance the crowd fell back and divided itself. The voices of the mob became hushed. He turned to her calmly, "So shall it be in the latter days."

With these words he walked unmolested through the crowd, and Venna, spell-bound, watched him go.

Then it was that she awoke with a confused idea of the reality of life.

Her aunt stood by her bed.

"Well, dearie, I've let you sleep as long as possible. You know we have an engagement with Madame Amelia at eleven o'clock. She won't finish your dress if you don't keep the appointment."

Venna jumped up, now fully awake.

"I'll be ready in half an hour, breakfast and all, auntie!"

"Very well, dear. I'll order the car promptly at 10:30."

Venna gave her aunt an impulsive hug.

"What a gay time we'll have to-morrow night!" she exclaimed, the girl in her quickly responding to the preparations for her debut.

Her aunt flushed with happiness.

"We are going to make it the best money can provide!" she returned with gentle affection and pride, as she left her niece to dress.

The entire morning was taken up in making calls upon dressmaker and florist and completing the already much talked over preparations.

Venna was excitedly happy and her aunt's quiet joy seemed like the reflection of the young life she was so devoted to.

However, when they returned home and had lunched, Venna found herself tired—the natural reaction asserted itself.

"Auntie, I think I'll disappear for an hour, and have a good rest. Then I'll be ready for anything."

"Very well, dear. Sleep as long as you wish. There is nothing for you to do now but dream of the good time coming. Everything is done."

So Venna went to her room, removed her dress, and for a moment stood undecided beside her open wardrobe.

There hung three pretty kimonos, one red, one blue, and one nile green. It was a peculiar little habit with Venna to don the color that best suited her mood at the time of wearing.

She always said that if she felt very tired, she liked the green. If she felt excitedly happy, she liked the red. If very thoughtful, the blue suited her best.

This time she stood hesitating and laughed softly.

"I really don't know which I want to wear, so guess my feelings are all hopelessly mixed."

Her hand finally reached out for the blue, and with the soft color wrapped about her pretty girlishness, she lay down to sleep.

Let us take a peep around this room. Everything Venna did or had was characteristic of her, and her own cosy room was no exception.

It was oblong in shape, with an open fireplace at one end and her carved mahogany bed at the other.

Along one wall, between two windows, stood her mahogany dresser and dressing table. On the other side, with a door at one end, stood first a mahogany book-case, then a mahogany work table covered with sewing bag and magazines, and next to this a large Victrola, ready to give its series of concerts. In the centre of the room was another mahogany table, covered with more books.

The wall paper was a subdued buff, and a dark oriental rug covered the floor. The window draperies were of cream lace, lambriquined with the palest blue silk.

A few choice pictures with uniform frames of black and gold gave the finishing touch to a room more suited to a library than a boudoir.

Venna's aunt often suggested a change of furnishings.

"White maple or anything more girlish would be better," she said.

But Venna's ideas were unchangeable.

"Mahogany always looks so real—that's why I like it best," she invariably replied.

Neither her father nor her aunt knew just exactly what she meant, but if mahogany was Venna's taste, the best of its kind should be hers.

Venna did not sleep long. She awoke rather unrefreshed and tired. She thought of her last night's peculiar dream, and with the thought came the desire to read the tracts the young preacher had given her.

Arising and opening her bag, she found there were only three—one on baptism, one on the Second Coming of Christ and one named "Rays of Living Light."

She sat in her luxurious easy chair by the window and was soon absorbed in thoughts quite new and interesting to her ever receptive mind.

Meantime her aunt downstairs was undergoing quite a shock.

A few minutes after Venna retired, her cousin Luella Allen called.

She was a tall, thin spinster who had never married because the love of her early youth had died. Have you ever met that kind, reader? I mean the one who constantly reminds you of by-gone sorrows with a sort of weepy allegiance to the past which is pious in the extreme and forbids the thought of too much joyousness in the present. Also there is an accompanying tendency to dampen the happiness of others.

Such was Luella Allen, and as she entered the room Emily Hastings noticed the suppressed twitching of her long, thin features and knew this was a sign of strong inward emotions.

The two women saluted one another with the usual formal kiss and seated themselves.

"What news now, Luella?" asked Emily calmly, for she knew without news Luella Allen seldom called.

"O Emily! I know all about it, dear! I've come to talk it over with you. I saw the whole thing. It's so shocking I can hardly believe it. We really must take Venna in hand and make her realize she is too grown up to act ridiculous now and disgrace us!"

Emily stiffened and flushed.

"I don't understand you, Luella. Venna couldn't disgrace anyone. She is as near perfect as any girl could be."

"Didn't John tell you then? The poor dear! He didn't want to shock you, did he? But I think you ought to know."

Here she paused and lifted her black bordered handkerchief to her nose to indulge in a sympathetic snuffle.

"Please explain, Luella!" Emily's voice was unusually impatient and short.

"Oh, I know John will blame me for telling you Emily, but I'll do my duty," she said righteously. "Last night I was on Broadway and in the crowd my car was stopped. I looked out of the window and I saw—I can scarcely believe it yet—I saw our Venna standing in the street with a handful of those wicked Mormons—(yes, I found out afterwards, they were Mormons)—playing her violin to a mixed New York crowd. Just think of it! *Our* Venna!"

Emily Hastings had suddenly paled.

"Luella, it can't be true! Where was John?"

"I don't know, Emily dear." Luella's tone now changed to one of complete satisfaction at desired results. "He must have been somewhere near and found it out. I always said Venna has her mother's impulsiveness. Of course, she didn't *mean* any harm—but think what might have come of it. Those Mormon preachers are in the East for only one purpose. You know that, Emily. Just to entice pretty girls like Venna to go to Utah to their destruction, and they use the cloak of religion, too! More's the shame. I'm so thankful the child is safe."

Emily's color had returned and burned each cheek.

"I'm sure, Luella, you are mistaken. I shall bring Venna here to tell you so," and Emily sailed from the room with a majestic disdain, quite uncommon to her quiet, even composure.

Gently she opened Venna's door.

"Should she awaken her? No, Luella must be crazy!" she thought disdainfully. Yet it might be true. Venna was so impulsive. However, there was no harm done. Venna was safe—she must be talked to, of course.

So quietly she closed the door and went back to the library.

"Venna is sleeping," she said, her mild self again. "Thank you, Luella, for telling me. I shall speak to John about it."

"Oh, I wish I could advise the dear girl myself!" Luella returned disappointed.

"I can't disturb her. These are very busy days in her young life."

Luella arose. "Then, Emily, I'll be going. I have an engagement myself, but just stepped in to warn you. The dear girl shall certainly have my prayers," she added, and with another formal kiss and good-bye, she was gone.

Emily Hastings took a deep breath. The air seemed freer for her going. Down in her heart, she disliked her cousin immensely, but John always said, "Be kind to her," and what John said, Emily did.

When Venna finished reading her tracts, she laid them upon the table and slowly began to dress. While so doing, she was very thoughtful.

Who were these good missionaries who had such interesting thoughts to pass around? She had heard of a very questionable "Mormon" Church in Utah—everyone knew them to be very immoral and treacherous, but how did these missionaries get connected with that Church and have these inspiring tracts? The more she thought about it, the more confusing it was. Surely here was a paradox! She was still wondering, when the door opened gently and her aunt entered.

"Are you going out, Venna? If not, I would like to talk with you awhile."

"No, I was just wishing to talk to you, auntie dear. I'm very puzzled about something. Do you know very much about the Mormon Church?"

Emily Hastings' face flushed as she met the girl's direct questioning gaze. "The idea of Luella Allen ever imagining Venna would hide anything," she thought indignantly.

"As much as I care to know, dear," she replied. "They are a very dangerous people, as everyone understands, and it is well to keep away from them. What possessed you to join them on Broadway? I can scarcely bear the thought of you doing anything like that."

"Did Daddy tell you about it? Really, auntie, I didn't know they were Mormons—I thought they were some good Christian missionaries. I don't know what possessed me. I just wanted to help the little girl who couldn't play her violin. But really, I can't think that young preacher is wicked. He seemed so earnest."

"Appearances are very deceptive, girlie," replied her aunt mildly, "Nothing good could come from the Mormons. Dr. Hansom paid a lecturer from Utah to come to tell us all about them. I don't remember all he said, but it was quite enough for me," she added complacently.

"I would like to talk to Dr. Hansom myself," Venna replied.

"You can this very afternoon. He will be here soon to talk with me about some improvements for the old ladies' home. He's so interested in all our charities. Such a wonderful man! There's the bell now. I guess that is he. As soon as you're dressed, come down, dear. I'm sure he will give you a few moments of his valuable time," and she left the room, happy in the thought that Dr. Hansom would talk seriously to Venna, and so prevent her ever being so reckless again.

When Venna had finished her toilet, complete in every dainty detail, she went downstairs.

As she reached the door of the library, with a bright "May I come in?" Dr. Hansom arose from his seat at the farther end of the room, and approached her with a genial smile.

"Ah! Venna! Come in. We're just talking about you!" he exclaimed, taking her hand and shaking it warmly, and then, placing her arm in his, he led her to a comfortable chair by the fire.

Dr. Hansom, short, thick-set, gray-eyed, with a determined stiff pompadour over a somewhat low-browed, broad face, had a way of doing everything genially. When he crossed a room it was with a free and easy swing, invariably with one hand in his pocket. When he walked down the avenue, his "hail-fellow-well-met" attitude toward all mankind was expressed in his free and careless stride. His smile, too, had a broadness and frankness quite irresistible to the majority and he was universally declared to possess a "wonderfully magnetic" character.

On a trolley car, he more often than not stood upon the platform and talked genially to the conductor, thus impressing all with his spirit of democracy.

In short. Dr. Hansom was one of the popular metropolitan ministers.

All the East knew of him, and his influence at mass meetings for men was a topic of great interest.

Men liked a man like Dr. Hansom. Consequently they fell in line with the religion he taught.

It was a practical, common-sense religion—founded upon the Bible, of course—but eliminating anything that the ordinary man of the day could not easily grasp.

Sin is an evil—he taught that. The consequences of sin, his oratorical powers set forth. This also was taking and helped men to determine to do better.

But when it came to the personality of Satan, the inspiration of the Old Testament, or the Second Coming of Christ, or numerous revelations and prophecies—all these subjects were hazy and too impractical to be discussed by the masses. Therefore Dr. Hansom dismissed them with a smile of inconsequence and assured the slumbering spirituality of his flock that there were more important things than the mysteries.

In this way Dr. Hansom avoided a great deal of real thinking and made many friends.

His large congregation of two thousand, including men, women and children, were all "Hansomized." What Dr. Hansom said went.

On the other hand, he was a mouthpiece for the sentiments of the general public.

His mind was like the disc of a phonograph, upon which public sentiment made an impress to be reproduced later from his pulpit at the inspiration of his desire to please.

Also he could be very stern and frankly abusive at times. But this, too, was part of the impression upon the disc, for the public enjoy strong censure and fearlessness.

They never realized this fine gift of Dr. Hansom's. Erroneously they thought he was original.

"I hear, Venna, you are puzzled about the Mormons?" he asked, sitting down opposite to her, and leaning slightly forward, placing both hands emphatically on the arms of his chair.

"Yes, Dr. Hansom. Are they really such awful people?" she asked seriously.

"Awful is no word for it, my girl. They are the most insidious menace in the religious world today! They lie, they lead immoral lives, and all under the cloak of religion! Your aunt told me of your indiscretion last night." Here he smiled indulgently. "Of course, we know our girl didn't realize what she was doing, but it ought to be a lesson to you. Never be led away with any sensational religion. You are liable to get trapped into anything if you do. I'm glad you are safe. But where was your father?"

Venna colored. "Father was not to blame. I did it before he realized what I was doing."

"Very true. You certainly took me by surprise, Venna," her father's voice laughingly exclaimed, and they all turned to see John Hastings enter the door, his keen eyes twinkling with amusement and cynicism.

"Ah, Hastings! I'm glad you joined us," exclaimed Dr. Hansom, jumping up and extending his hand. "We were telling Venna what the Mormons really are!"

"Umph! And what *really* are they?" he asked, as he seated himself with the group.

Dr. Hansom was always slightly less confident when talking to Hastings. He had a vague idea that here was one man in his Church whose ideas he did not exactly reflect. However, they were excellent friends.

"Why, Hastings, you don't have to ask that, do you? Didn't our lecture satisfy you concerning them?"

"No man's lecture satisfies me concerning any sect," returned Hastings quietly.

"But it is not one man's opinion, Hastings. All Christendom is against them," urged Dr. Hansom.

Venna looked from one to the other, intently listening.

Her aunt flushed with mild annoyance. Surely John was spoiling Dr. Hansom's influence over Venna.

Hastings leaned back in his chair with an air of boredom.

"How all the sects do enjoy biting and snapping at any new thing in their midst. Why doesn't each one live and let live?" he asked quietly.

"You don't mean you wish to defend the Mormons?" Dr. Hansom asked impatiently.

"Defend? No, neither do I mean to criticize. We in the East know very little about them, except what paid lecturers tell us, and that is rather 'commercialized truth,' don't you think?"

"Is it not an established fact that women influenced by Mormon missionaries have gone to Utah to their destruction?" persisted Dr. Hansom.

"Haven't the slightest doubt of it," was Hastings' smiling answer. "Also, it is an established fact that women have fallen in love with some Orthodox ministers and even Catholic priests, and followed them to their destruction. That doesn't denounce the Church politic, does it? There are black sheep in every fold."

Dr. Hansom frowned. He hated contradiction.

"I tell you, Hastings, the Mormons are outside of any fold—they are a menace that every Christian should strive to wipe off the map of this country!"

Hastings made no reply, but Venna spoke up confidently.

"Dr. Hansom, you certainly know more about these people than I do, but I'm *sure* that young preacher we met last night is sincere and good."

"How do you know? You scarcely spoke to him."

"O, but don't you think there are some people you meet, you just simply *feel* are good?"

"There you are, my dear girl," replied her pastor, with a deprecatory wave of the hand. "Led by your emotional nature again! If you don't stifle that tendency, Venna, it will get you into all kinds of trouble."

Venna's direct gaze was unwavering. "I don't say this from any emotion, Dr. Hansom, but Paul says, 'Spiritual things are spiritually discerned' and I felt his spirituality in his look and tone of voice."

"Doubtless you *thought* you did," returned Dr. Hansom, a little taken aback. "But you are a very young girl to have such decided ideas about spiritual matters. It would be wise to trust to those who have had more experience."

Hastings' brow contracted as he gazed intently into the fire without comment.

Dr. Hansom noticed his expression and disliked his silence, both of which had disconcerted him before.

He arose to go.

"I must be off now," he said. "Just six more calls to make this afternoon and then I suppose I'll find a number waiting for me at the Parish house when I return." He smiled a happy smile of genial importance, and after the usual hearty hand-shakes was gone.

Aunt Emily hid her disappointment in John's behavior by a quiet exit.

Now alone with her father, Venna drew her chair close to his and laid her small hand on his big, strong one.

He turned his gaze affectionately upon her.

"A little child shall lead them," he thought, but did not say. After all, it was wiser for Venna not to rely too much upon her own discernment.

"Girlie," he said aloud, "don't be governed too much by appearances. As Dr. Hansom says, you might go woefully adrift in your judgements."

"But, Daddy, don't you think that young preacher was sincere?" she persisted.

"I don't think about it, dear," he returned practically. "He might be or he might not be. Just leave all questionable people alone and stick to your Church, which you know is about as good as you'll find these days."

And so the subject was dismissed, but when Venna returned to her room she took the tracts and carefully put them in a drawer which held her special treasures.

"I *know* he is God's man," she said softly, as she laid them away.

CHAPTER II.

In the full glare of the dazzling footlights of social life, we are blinded to the softer, purer rays that proceed from the "holy of holies" within our hearts.

John Hastings' Fifth Avenue mansion was ablaze with light. He had cautioned his servants, smilingly,

"Don't let one electric bulb be forgotten in any nook of our home to-night. There must be an abundance of brightness!"

The servants promised gaily, and went about their several duties with a delight, not only the result of high wages and exceptional treatment, but because each one individually loved Venna with a respectful adoration.

The long reception rooms were one garden of palms and roses.

As Venna stood by the side of her aunt, under a canopy of green, her silvered white dress sparkling as she moved, her beauty was never so enchanced. So thought her social friends, as one by one they approached to shake hands and congratulate the radiant debutante.

The hidden orchestra, screened by palms, played dreamy music while Venna beamed happy and smiled upon her delighted guests.

"Was I ever so happy?" she asked herself joyously.

There were several men who lingered unnecessarily over their congratulations, and with each occurrence Venna laughed to herself.

She knew how much they admired her and it seemed delightfully amusing. As yet, love was no serious consideration in her life.

But now almost the last one entered—a man of thirty, dark, with handsome straight features and very upright bearing.

As he took her hand, his direct gaze was very compelling.

"This occasion. Miss Hastings, is, I hope, the beginning of a better acquaintance with one another."

The words were very simple, but the look said much more, and the firm pressure of her hand was hardly necessary.

She had met him only once before. Why should she blush? Her admirer noticed her embarrassment with satisfaction.

"Yes, I hope so, Mr. Hadly," she said simply, withdrawing her hand as soon as she politely could.

"May I have the first dance?" he asked, still compelling her gaze.

She laughingly handed him her card.

"See! There is only one left—right near the last, too!"

"Ah! That is my punishment for being late! Well, that one will furnish my anticipated joy for the whole evening," he returned, writing his name on the card and handing it to her reluctantly. Then he passed on to make room for Dr. Hansom and his wife who were next in turn.

"Dear me! Is this little sparkling lady my little Venna grown old enough to enter society! It seems just yesterday when I took you in my arms and baptized you, Venna Hastings!"

His thin, mild little wife smiled and nodded, with a gentle "That's so, Venna!"

"Eighteen long, long years. Dr. Hansom," said Venna gaily.

"Eighteen long, long years in which nature has labored to produce one of the most beautiful and talented young artists in New York City!" exclaimed Dr. Hansom, turning and speaking in a distinct voice for all to hear him.

At this the whole assemblage clapped loudly and Venna bowed her acceptance.

Oh, the dance! The delight of it! As soon as Venna was released from the formalities, her feet were gliding over the polished floor with a lightness corresponding to her joyous mood.

One by one her partners claimed her for their succeeding numbers, each one reluctantly giving her up to the next one in turn.

Mr. Hadly was constantly on the floor also. He was the most graceful dancer among the men. Though politely attentive to his partners, Venna felt his gaze constantly upon herself, and several times blushed as she met his ardent look of admiration.

She was quite surprised with herself to think that any man could make her so self-conscious.

Finally came the dance promised to Mr. Hadly. He approached her smiling.

"I wonder if you would like to sit this out in the conservatory," he said in a tone which asked her to do so.

They were soon seated among the palms and Venna leaned back among the cushions with a sigh of happiness.

"You have been radiantly happy this evening, haven't you?" he asked softly.

"And how could I *not* be?" she asked, smiling.

"Very true. The freshness of youth commands happiness."

How alluring she was to this man of the world!

"I won't have long with you to-night—just these passing moments of one dance. I want you to set a date when I may call. I have your father's permission, Miss Hastings. After I have called, then I wish to beg you to allow me to escort you to a number of social functions this winter, that I know will be worth while. Your dancing is wonderful. I'm very fond of the art myself. I think we ought to be very good partners."

He surveyed her from head to foot with keen appreciation.

Venna felt his thoughts. Surely, it was pleasure to be admired by this handsome man of affairs. She was getting accustomed to him now, and her embarrassment had left her. She looked up pleased.

"I'm ready for good times this winter. Father insists on me enjoying life— for a time anyway."

"For a time anyway?" he repeated. "Why not always?" he asked, studying her intently.

"Oh, one couldn't take life *always* as a holiday," she brightly returned.

"As long as one can," he replied, his eyes slightly darkening. "The good time is here if you know how to get it. There! I've hardly had time to speak to you and the music is stopping. You haven't told me when I shall call."

Venna appointed the evening and then together they returned to the dance.

When supper was served, Venna found Mr. Hadly sitting directly opposite to her. He used his opportunity well, and compelled her to meet his glance many times even when she was talking to others.

"How handsome he is!" she thought. "And such a forcible character, too."

He certainly attracted Venna more than any of her gentlemen friends. Yet with the attraction, she felt a slight repulsion she could not understand.

—

The wonderful evening over, and the guests departed, Venna stood alone with her father under the green canopy where she had received her friends.

Her cheeks were flushed and her eyes as bright as in the early evening. No sign of fatigue was evident.

"O Daddy, I could have danced all night!" she exclaimed happily.

"Some success, wasn't it, dearie?" he returned, putting his arm lovingly around her. "Now, I suppose this winter will be one whirl of gayety for you."

"Nothing will ever be just quite as nice as this, Daddy," she said, kissing him. "I'll never, never, never forget it!"

"We wouldn't want you to, Venna," he replied, immensely pleased. "By the way, I noticed you have a new admirer."

Venna blushed.

"Whom do you mean?" she asked with assumed unconcern.

"Mr. Hadly, of course. He's one of New York's rich catches. It seems the girls have been after him for some years, but he isn't caught yet. A nice sort of fellow, but—understand, young lady, you don't give your heart away for some time yet. Daddy's too selfish."

"Never fear. Daddy! It'll be a very long time before that happens; Daddy's enough for me." And her arms stole around his neck in an impulsive hug.

And so we will leave them in their oneness of heart, father and daughter, inseparable in their sweet companionship until a higher power shall sever their lives.

CHAPTER III.

"In the midst of life is death."

It was a warm, sultry day in early April. The Hastings family were just settled in their summer home in Allendale. Venna had been "to town" all the morning on a shopping expedition, and had returned home somewhat fatigued by the warmth of the early spring. She had lunched and was resting alone in her room. She sat by her open window with her book in her lap, unheeded. Her head resting back upon the cushions, she dreamily watched the robins busying themselves with nest building in the tree outside.

"Poor little birds!" she mused. "You're working so hard for your little home and the first storm may blow it down!"

The robins continued to chirp happily.

"You'll be happy anyway while it lasts," she thought, "and if your nest falls, you'll build another—just as we all do!"

Venna certainly was in a dreamy mood. Her mind wandered over the entire winter's doings, since her debut.

Her debut! How well she remembered the keen enjoyment of it! But the months following! Had she found them all satisfying? She had to admit that she had not. One whirl of gayety had been hers. She had been the acknowledged belle of the season. Among her many admirers, Mr. Hadly pushed himself always to the front and assumed "the right of way" with such firmness that her friends took it for granted that it would culminate in a brilliant match. Venna did not repulse, neither did she encourage, him. She was so busy having "a good time" that she let admiration take its course and if the other men were so easily pushed aside, Venna did not care. She liked Hadly's masterful way of doing things. If he invited her anywhere, it was always in a manner which said, "You'll be sorry if you don't go." And she had to admit that his invitations resulted in the most pleasurable times of the winter.

"Am I in love with him?" she asked herself today, as she had many times before.

"No, decidedly not!" was her answer, which always pleased herself, for Venna didn't want to be in love yet, and be married like all the other girls who had gone out ahead of her. She wanted "to do something" first. Just what she meant to "do" she hadn't decided, but the married girls she knew led such monotonous lives—society, society and always the same dressing, entertaining and being entertained.

It was plain Venna's one year in the social world was enough. Yes, she had tired of it already. She was going to talk to Daddy about it. Next year, she would like to play at real public concerts—not just social functions—and really earn money. But why earn money? Daddy had an endless supply on hand for her always.

Well, maybe she could do settlement work. She had a friend who was immensely interested in it. She had met her only lately and the girl said she was never so happy as when working among the poor.

"I believe that's what I'll do," she exclaimed, and her eyes lost their dreaminess and shone brightly.

There was a sudden chirping of the robins and Venna looked out.

The clouds had gathered and a strong wind was blowing. The tree swayed to and fro. The little half finished nest fell from its bough, down, down, until it was lost to view.

"Poor little birds!" thought Venna, as she watched them fly away, chirping excitedly.

Suddenly a great depression stole over her and she began to cry softly.

"What is the matter with me?" she exclaimed, wiping away her tears with determination. "Why should I have this sudden sadness? I must not give way to it."

She arose and closed her window, for the rain was coming down quite heavily. It grew suddenly dark. Venna pulled down her shades, put the lights on, and started to dress.

"I must get busy and shake off this uncalled for mood before Daddy comes home. He may take an early train and will be coming home tired from the hot city. There's the car now!"

But it was not her father. The maid announced "Mr. Hadly," as she handed Venna a long box.

"Please open it, Stella. I'll be ready to wear one, I guess."

The maid opened up the gift of American Beauties—Venna's favorites—and handed one long stemmed rose to her mistress.

"Put the rest in water, Stella—I shall wear only one," she said, pinning the wonderful rose at her waist. "And when you go to your party to-night, just come in and take one for yourself," she added kindly.

"Oh, thank you, miss," exclaimed the maid, as she helped Venna with her dress. "You do just look wonderful today, Miss Venna. Your cheeks are as red as the rose itself."

Venna was always so familiar with her servants and they were frankly adoring.

"Thank you, my dear Stella," she said. "Your compliments have a sameness, but I always know they are sincere," she said, as she left the room to go to her guest.

Hadly awaited Venna in the large reception room facing the front porch. He looked about the cozy room all in oak and cool green, and then at the centre table with vases of violets and apple-blossoms.

He smiled as he looked at the flowers. He had a bright vision of Venna gathering them and placing them there.

Venna entered the room with her usual bright smile.

"You arrived just in time, Mr. Hadly. We are in for a storm, I guess. How dark it is!"

A sudden flash of lightning and clap of thunder made them both start.

Venna hastily put on the lights with a slight shiver.

"Let us pull down the shades, too," she said. "It doesn't seem so bad then."

"Are you afraid of a thunder-storm. Miss Hastings?" he asked as he shut out the storm.

"Not ordinarily," she returned, suddenly paling as another streak of lightning penetrated the room, followed by thunder that shook the house.

Hadly crossed to her side, and taking her arm gently, led her to a chair.

"You really look pale. Tell me, there is something more than the storm that has frightened you. What is it?"

"I don't know," returned Venna, sitting down. "I was watching the robins outside my window when I was possessed with an indescribable sadness. It passed off and now comes this fear. I don't understand it. I never fear a storm."

He stood beside her chair, towering handsomely by her side. He looked down into her face so full of questioning fear. Surely now was his time.

"Miss Hastings—Venna—may I call you Venna? because you have never feared a storm in the past is not to say you never will. Won't you give me the privilege of sheltering you from all the storms of the future? Venna, I love you. Not with the half love of a youth, but with the strong love of a matured manhood that knows the world and can therefore appreciate a girl like you the more."

He leaned over her but did not touch her. His eyes seemed to burn their passion into her very soul and for a moment held her spell-bound.

She might have expected this, yet she had drifted on. Now she was suddenly confronted with the passionate love of a man who was in dead earnest and evidently expected a return. Feeling the embarrassment of refusing him, she dropped her eyes in confusion.

He took her hand and pressed it hard.

"You will then be my wife, Venna?"

The same masterful way he expected her to accept him. What could she say?

"You *do* love me?" he again insisted.

She finally gained courage and raised her eyes to meet his with frank regret.

"Mr. Hadly, I wish that I could love a man like you, for I know your love is one for any girl to be proud of. I know you are sincere in caring for me. But I don't think it is in me to love any man—not *yet*, I am sure."

His eyes darkened with disappointment.

"Then I have been deceived all this time—thinking you surely loved me as you have accepted my attentions unreservedly."

Venna blushed with conscious shame.

"I had no reason to believe you"—there she stopped short. She was not yet accustomed to handle proposals. She felt a quick self-blame. She had enjoyed herself at this man's expense.

He read her thoughts.

"There, Venna, I do not blame you. You are very young. I must not expect too much love at first. Just say that you will marry me!"

"Without loving you?" she asked in sudden wonder.

"Why not?" he asked, smiling into her eyes. "Once we are married, I will teach you to love."

He leaned so near to her now that his breath was upon her cheek. She felt he was about to kiss her. She withdrew from him with a sudden repulsion.

"Don't!" she said, imploringly. "I never could love you—nor any other man," she added, childishly, finding words to make the hurt seem less.

At this moment Stella appeared at the door.

"Telegram, Miss," she said. "An immediate answer wanted."

Hadly covered Venna's confusion by walking over to Stella, taking the telegram and handing it to Venna, who mechanically took it.

"Thank you, Stella. I will call you when I have the answer ready."

The maid quietly withdrew.

Hastily Venna opened the telegram.

As she read, her face paled and the telegram dropped from her trembling hands. Rigid she sat gazing before her with fixed stare.

"Venna! What is it? Tell me!" insisted Hadly.

She did not answer him, but the look of sudden anguish on the girl's face made him take up the telegram and read.

"John Hastings met with serious accident at 2:30 today. Now at the M— Hospital. Come at once. Cannot live many hours."

A sudden look of relief crept into his handsome face, but it was instantly replaced by one of compassion for the girl before him.

"You poor girl," he said, kneeling beside her and, placing both arms around her inert form, he drew her gently to him.

In her stormy grief, Venna's power of resistance was gone. She knew she was suffering keenly; but without definitely realizing the cause. But Hadly's caresses soon brought her to her full senses, and she withdrew from his arms in great anxiety.

"Your car is here. Can you take me to the train immediately?"

"I will take you to New York, right to the hospital, dear," was his ready answer.

"Thank you!" she exclaimed excitedly. "But, auntie—how can we tell her?"

"Is she home?"

"No, she went out this morning for a long ride with the Jetsons. They are probably caught in the storm somewhere. It will be impossible to find her. We must not lose the next train," she exclaimed, glancing hurriedly at her watch which pointed to 3:30.

"When do you expect her home?"

"Maybe not until six o'clock dinner. Oh, we must hurry!"

"Yes, by that time we can be in New York. Get your things quickly. Your aunt must follow. Ring for Stella. I will explain to her while you get ready."

Venna found her excitement giving way to a great calm. As oil thrown upon an angry sea stills the turbulent waters, so a great unseen influence pervaded the girl's being and quieted the tempest of her mind. She could not understand it, but was thankful.

Her great pallor startled the maid as they met at the door.

"Stella, Mr. Hadly will explain. I am hurrying to catch the next train to New York."

With these words, she ran upstairs, entered her room, and quickly dressed for the city. Before leaving, she stood for a moment in front of her father's picture, smiling down upon her.

"O God, help me!" she exclaimed piteously, but her eyes were tearless.

She quickly rejoined Hadly and together they started in his closed limousine. The storm had somewhat abated, but it still rained hard, and lightning continually flashed in upon them.

Protectingly he put his arm around her. She did not withdraw. It seemed natural now. She needed someone, anyone, to accompany her in her grief.

"How kind he is!" she thought, vaguely realizing this hour of trial was drawing them closer together.

Venna never fully remembered what was said on that trip to New York. Her mind was full of longing to get to her father, and she answered Hadley's constant remarks in monosyllables, scarcely realizing what he said.

His whole attitude was one of protecting ownership. So they rushed on to the great city which was to hold her first awful sorrow.

Love for her father was the only affection she was capable of feeling now, but Hadly was asking nothing. He was giving all. She had a dim appreciation of his kindness, and thanked him several times. Each time he refused her thanks with an ardent declaration that his only object in life was to serve her always.

At last the awful journey was over. The train drew into the Grand Central and a taxi then took them hurriedly to the hospital.

Venna's calmness was even more pronounced as they approached the desk and asked for "John Hastings."

She scarcely breathed as the doctor took up the hospital phone.

Then the cold reply was brusquely given: "All right, you can go right up."

Silently they followed the orderly, Venna leading with a firm, light step.

As they entered the room where her father lay, Venna stood still and gazed with horror at what she saw. Was this her own beloved Daddy? There upon the couch lay a man with the pallor of death making more ghastly the two awful gashes on cheek and forehead.

The nurse attending held up a finger of silence and approached her kindly.

"Don't disturb him," she whispered. "He will doubtless awaken soon."

Approaching the bed noiselessly, Venna sat down upon the chair placed for her.

Hadly walked over to the window and looked out with a grim expression, avoiding too close a contact with death.

As spirit communes with spirit, so Venna's presence brought back the consciousness of her father. He opened his eyes slowly and fastened them upon her with unutterable joy.

"My darling girl, you have come!" he murmured, making a weak effort to lift his hand.

She leaned gently over him and kissed his white lips.

"Yes, Daddy, I'm here, dear. I'm here to stay with you until you go home," she said quietly but with a voice full of love.

His eyes saddened.

"Until—I go—home, dearie? That will be soon, very soon. Be sure you stay."

His eyes closed again in sudden weakness.

Venna stared at him in horror.

"Daddy, daddy, you don't mean—Oh! speak to me. Daddy!" she cried piteously.

His eyes opened once more and smiled upon her, full of loving concern.

"Venna child, be brave," he whispered. "I'm going home-to your dear mother. Be brave. Be—good, Petty. Always—be—good, for—Daddy's sake. See Venna! There is your mother now. Look! She comes! O beautiful wife!"

He said no more. His eyes, lit with a holy joy, looked beyond Venna.

Suddenly he raised both arms outstretched in welcome. Then they fell. His eyes dimmed.

"Daddy!" cried Venna in anguish.

But there was no answer. Venna was alone.

CHAPTER IV.

Life is measured, not by time, but by experience.

Her father's sudden death left Venna an heiress, but never having known anything but luxury, she did not value her wealth. In fact, it might have been a considerable burden to both Venna and her aunt, both of whom were entirely ignorant of business, but Mr. Hadly took everything in hand, attending to details, and leaving as little as possible to the lawyers. This, he assured them, was the only safe way, and gratefully they accepted his services.

Both Venna and Emily Hastings were almost inconsolable in their grief. The latter found some consolation in Dr. Hansom's visits, but to Venna these were no comfort. She naturally turned to him, but his faith was the kind that handled the world's troubles *en masse*, and in personal grief, he had few words to say.

Venna asked him many questions about the hereafter, to which he gave many vague answers.

"It is not for us to know anything definitely. Faith leaves it all to God," he assured her in conclusion.

"But surely the Bible gives us some certainties, Dr. Hansom," she pleaded, hungry for spiritual truths.

"So much depends on how you interpret the Bible, my dear. I declare very few certainties to my people, because there are very brainy men who all differ. Of course there's a hereafter, and your father was a good member of the Church, so we know he is happy. I'm very glad he joined the Church before it was too late."

"Do you mean my dear father would not have been saved if he had *not* joined the Church?" Venna asked credulously.

Dr. Hansom had to clear his throat before answering.

"Really, my dear, I don't like to hurt you. I loved your dear father always, but if he had not joined himself to the House of the Lord, I would be forced to believe he was lost."

"Then God loved my father less than you or I did—we wouldn't see him lost, would we? Oh, Dr. Hansom, religion teaches many a paradox today. I don't wonder there is so little spirituality in the Churches."

Dr. Hansom turned the subject with a fatherly pat of her curls and the admonition,

"Don't judge, little girl, don't judge. There may be a hidden life in the Church which you cannot see!"

But Venna decided the "hidden life" brought her no satisfaction or comfort and gradually she drifted away from the Church.

Hadly took this opportunity to show his devotion at every turn.

Her aunt thought him about perfect and spoke in his praise continually.

Venna acquiesced in all she said, but for a long time refused to marry him. However, he had determined to win out and persisted constantly, asking no love of Venna in return for his.

At last her aunt's persuasions and Hadly's determination won out, and one year after her father's death, they were quietly married. Venna felt a certain satisfaction that she was delighting her aunt and also making happy the greatest friend she had known through her sorrow.

Many times she puzzled over the fact that her coldness did not worry Hadly at all. But she decided that men were unfathomable in their affections, and such devotion as his was certainly noble. She wished she could love him— perhaps some day she would.

She made all kinds of plans for her married life. Hadly had promised to let her work among the poor to her heart's content. No plan of hers ever met with the slightest objection, and her aunt continually reminded her what an ideal husband he was.

"But am I an ideal wife?" Venna asked doubtfully.

"Anyone should be glad to win *you*, dearie," was always her aunt's proud answer.

She longed to live in the old home, so Hadly, as usual, consented.

It was just six months after her marriage.

Venna was in the dear old library sorting out some books to use in her settlement work. Her husband's business caused him to travel so much that she had practically all her time to herself. After all, her married life had been a very smooth, contented affair.

When at home, her husband was completely devoted to Venna and her aunt. But when he was away she felt a joyous relief at her freedom and worked with zeal.

It never occurred to her to inquire into his many business trips. All business was a bore to her, and she was glad to leave it entirely in his hands. She hoped she would never show her pleasure at his absence, for she earnestly longed to please him as he deserved.

Today she was rather wishing her husband were home. There were some important business details to be attended to and she needed his advice. But this trip would be an unusually long one for him. He had written only this morning that he could not be home for another week.

Just as she finished her work in the library, Stella brought in a card announcing a caller—"Miss Hedgeway."

"But I don't know her, Stella," said Venna, wonderingly. "Ask her her business, please."

Stella obeyed and soon returned with the short reply, "Very personal. That's all she would say."

"That is the method all the agents use. Tell her I'm sorry, but too busy today to see strangers."

"All right, ma'am," replied the girl.

Venna left the library and was going upstairs when she heard voices below.

"I tell you I *must* see her. It's important. I won't leave this house until you take me to Mrs. Hadly."

"But, madam, I have to obey orders. She refuses to see anyone at present."

"Tell your mistress what I say," came the confident answer.

Stella ascended the stairs reluctantly and Venna met her half way.

"I heard her, Stella. I will see her for a few moments—in the library."

"You wish to see me?" Venna asked pleasantly as she re-entered the library.

The woman, still standing, eyed Venna from head to foot critically before speaking.

Venna had the impression of a rather good looking, stout brunette with small, restless dark eyes. She was fashionably dressed, with a style more attractive than refined.

"So you are Mrs. Hadly!" she exclaimed rather than asked.

"I am Mrs. Hadly," replied Venna with dignity, "Why did you wish so to see me?"

"When you know what I have to say, you'll be glad you let me speak with you," the woman replied in a low, even tone. "Are we entirely alone? Sit near to me, please," she added, seating herself and drawing a chair close to her own for Venna.

"Is your business so private?" Venna asked curiously, as she seated herself, calmly amused at her visitor's impertinence.

The woman's face softened.

"You look rather young and innocent. I thought somehow you would be different. More like one of the haughty society women who wouldn't cast a glance at anyone outside their set!"

"All society women are not so," returned Venna, smiling. "But why should you picture *me* like that?"

"Only as his wife," the woman replied bitterly. "You're not his style, believe me. But the money did it—always the money does it."

"I don't understand you," returned Venna, rising indignantly. "If you have come here to insult me, whatever your motive, I must ask you to leave."

The woman rose, too, and laid a hand on Venna's arm.

"I tell you, I'm sorry for you. I don't want to hurt a girl like you. But now I'm here, I'll have it out. I came to hurt *him*, not you. I hate him. You understand? I *hate* him. I gave him five years of my youth, and we—yes, your husband and myself—have a little girl. I loved him—my God! How I loved him! I gave him more than *you* ever gave. And then he threw me over to marry *money*. Not you, girl, but your money! And I searched him out. I came to New York to find his wife and ruin *him*. Here, girl! Don't take it so hard; sit down. You're faint, aren't you? I'm sorry I let it out so blunt. I should have gone easier—yes, you've got to suffer, too, poor thing!" And she put her arm around Venna for support.

But Venna, recovering, drew herself up haughtily.

"How dare you come here with such falsehoods!" she exclaimed indignantly. "Leave my house at once."

"That is how we all act, until we find out what men really are," replied the woman with a scornful pity. "It's hard to wake up to what the world really is, isn't it? Perhaps you don't think I'm sorry for you!"

"I will not listen to you," exclaimed Venna proudly. "Will you please go?"

The woman scrutinized Venna keenly. "No, you are not acting," she said coolly. "You'd rather believe in *him* than in *me*—naturally. But he'll soon run through all your money as he did his own, and then you'll be glad to have me tell you a little more about your ideal. Here is my card," she added, laying one upon the table. "I will come when you send for me," and with a smile, half contempt, half compassion, she was gone.

For a moment, Venna stood, deep in troubled thought. Who was this woman? What did it all mean? As her anger cooled, awful doubts crept into her mind and she trembled with fear. Could there be any truth in it? Had she been unwise not to listen? Yet that would have been treachery to Will. But suppose—she heard her aunt's voice calling her. Hastily she put the woman's card in her dress.

"Auntie must not know of this," she determined. A dull, heavy depression seized her. This was her first experience with a hidden trial, for trial it would be until Will could explain—of course, he would explain—but she would have to ponder over the mystery of it for a week.

It seemed unbearable. She decided to write to Will and ask him to come sooner.

She took up a pen and tried to write, but couldn't. Was it not wrong to doubt him that much even? Was it possible she could be so disloyal? In her self-condemnation, she was as unhappy as in her doubt.

Unobserved, her aunt entered.

"Why, Venna, how troubled you look! What is the matter, child?"

Venna was startled. Calm and pale, she faced her aunt.

"Nothing much, auntie dear. My head bothers me to-day, and there are some business details that need attending to."

"Business? Why, don't worry over that. Will will attend to everything when he returns."

"Yes, of course, it's foolish of me to bother," returned Venna. Her aunt's complete trust seemed to make her feel surer ground.

Emily Hastings, putting both arms around her niece, kissed her fondly.

"Girlie dear, I have a great secret to tell you," she said, gently smiling, her mild face flushed.

"At last?" asked Venna, smiling back knowingly.

One month after John Hastings' death. Dr. Hansom had lost his faithful little wife. It was a real sorrow to the great preacher, for not many women were to be found with a character so suited to meet all his requirements in a wife. After her death, he was a very frequent visitor at the old Hastings house. Gradually it dawned upon him that the mild, gentle Emily Hastings had a temperament most wonderfully like the dear woman he had lost. She was so unaggressive, so gentle, so adoringly submissive to whomsoever she loved. She would make a fine minister's wife.

It didn't take Dr. Hansom long to make up his mind. He doubled his attentions and visits, keeping silence, however, until the proper time had elapsed.

And now the wonderful hour had come.

It seemed an impossible joy laid at Emily Hastings' feet.

"If only your dear father could know!" she exclaimed, looking young in her new happiness.

"He does," returned Venna softly. "He knows all that happens to us," she added with a sudden pang at the thought of her own trouble.

"But, dearie. Dr. Hansom wishes us to marry very soon—of course, it will be a very quiet wedding. Do you think it is too soon?"

"No," returned Venna, lovingly patting her aunt's cheek. "The sooner you are made happy the better. I shall certainly hurry you off!"

"O Venna, if you were not married, I would never leave you. But now you have such a perfect husband, and he must give up his traveling when I go. I wouldn't have you lonesome for the world. Of course, we'll see one another all the time, but it won't seem just like living together, will it?"

Looking around the old familiar room her eyes suddenly filled with tears.

"Every rose has its thorn, but let's forget the sting and think only of the joy of it all," replied Venna, bravely choking back a sob.

There is a time in every girl's life when she finds herself suddenly a woman. The time of this change from girlhood to womanhood is not marked by the marriage ceremony. No, the period of happy girlhood extends to that time when some sharp experience awakens her soul to the realities of life. Then the illusions vanish and the woman in her lives. Not less capable of joy does she become, but absolutely and forever lost to the fantastic, unreal dreams of early youth.

Venna's awakening came simultaneously with her aunt's rejuvenating engagement announcement, which occurred one week after Dr. Hansom's proposal.

As soon as Hadly returned, Venna lost no time in asking him for an explanation of Miss Hedgeway's visit.

At first he denied knowing the woman, but his nervousness convinced his wife that he was not telling the truth.

"Will," she said, suddenly indignant, "if you do not tell me the truth, I shall find it out myself. What is this woman to you?"

He had never seen scorn in her eyes before and it was confoundedly unpleasant. Quickly he decided there was only one way—to make a clean breast of it.

"Yes, Venna," he said, frankly, "I have lied to you,—because I didn't like to destroy your innocent trust in me. She's *nothing* to me now, but she *was* an escapade of the past. I treated her fair enough—she always had money of her own—never wanted for anything. I didn't deceive her—she went into it with her eyes open like all those women do—I never deceived *any* woman. It was just a case of give and take. She's meaner than I thought to rake up a man's past before his wife's eyes. As a rule, they don't do that sort of thing."

He paused for a moment, but Venna made no remark. She was earnestly listening to his every word.

"Now, my dear," he continued more confidently, "you have, of course, always been sheltered so by your father, that you are ignorant of life in many respects. Please don't think your husband a monstrosity. I'm no better than the next man—no worse, either. I've lived in the world, seen all sides of it, too, but that is why I am all the more able to appreciate a girl like you—by contrast, you know, dear."

"I suppose, then, there were other women, too?" Venna demanded in a sharp, unnatural voice.

"Don't use that tone, Venna," he said impatiently. "It isn't like you. It's not becoming. Yes, I'll treat you fair and hide nothing. My extreme youth was rather wild, but that's all past now. From the day I first called upon you, I've led a clean, straight life—that was my duty toward you."

Venna gave a hard little laugh.

"What about your duty toward the other women?" she asked coldly.

"I don't understand you," he replied angrily. "If you are going to play censor with me, young lady, you have the wrong party. I've been frank with you, which every man is not, and you return it with rudeness."

Without a word Venna quietly arose and left the room.

"Well, if women aren't incorrigible!" he exclaimed in disgust, lighting a cigarette to calm his perturbed thoughts.

Venna sought her own room, dismayed at her state of mind. She felt as though some one had roughly shaken her and awakened her from the dream of one world to the stern realities of another.

With the awakening came an alarming disgust and hatred for her husband. She stood alone, reasoning, struggling with her new thoughts. Her ideas, at first confused, began to shape themselves definitely and bitterly. Three hours later she came from her room, a pale, determined woman.

When she calmly informed Hadly that from then on they would be as entire strangers, his first sensation of genuine surprise gave way to angry fear.

"You're not going to make fools of both of us, are you? What on earth are you making such a fuss about? Are you looking for a divorce? You can't get one. I'll tell you that right now. And your business affairs are tight in my hands, so don't try to be *too* independent."

"You refuse to let me go?" asked Venna, pale but unwavering.

"You can go anywhere and everywhere you please," he returned with sarcasm. "Considering what a loving wife you've been, the parting of the ways will not be so difficult to bear. But I warn you, if you make a fool of me in society by repeating this foolish gossip—even to your aunt—it won't go easy with you."

"Never fear," returned Venna bitterly. "No one shall suffer but myself. It is plain to be seen you will not. I shall leave town for the summer as soon as aunt is married, in a few weeks. As to money matters my lawyer will consult you."

Venna ostensibly busied herself with her aunt's rushed preparations for her quiet wedding, and Hadly found occasion to disappear on another business trip.

With the advent of her womanhood, came the power to smile and laugh with a breaking heart, and to hide from all her friends her sadness and trial.

The heart of a girl is easily read, but the heart of a woman is a hidden mystery.

CHAPTER V.

Just be glad that you are living and keep cheering someone on.

Venna sat alone at lunch, idly toying with her food. Stella busied herself around her mistress, offering first one thing and then another, with real concern in her honest face.

"Excuse me, ma'am, but you've hardly eaten anything since your aunt went away. You're right pale, you are."

"Am I?" returned Venna with a feeble smile. "I guess I must be going to the country soon. The fresh air makes me hungry."

"It's a warm day now, ma'am. John says, don't you want to use the car this afternoon?" Stella ventured anxiously.

"No, Stella, I don't want to go out today," she replied dully. "I don't think I care for any lunch either. You fixed everything so nice, too. I'll try to do better next time."

She arose from the table and was about to leave the room when she turned at the door.

"Stella, if anyone comes, remember I'm out—unless it's Mrs. Halloway. She wrote she would be home from the West any day. I'll see *her*."

"All right, ma'am."

But Stella shook her head as Venna disappeared.

"There's something wrong somewhere," she said to herself sadly. "She looks like a wilted flower. It's a dull old house with her father dead, her aunt married, and her husband traveling. But that doesn't account for her looking as though life was all entirely over, the poor dear!"

Venna went to her room and threw herself upon her couch in real despair.

Two weeks ago her aunt left the old home, a happy but tearful bride. Venna played her role, and smiled gaily until the time of parting was over, when she found herself alone with the servants in the once happy home of her girlhood. That was two weeks ago. It seemed like two years.

Her aunt's wedding trip was to be a joyous extended affair—she probably would be away three months.

Hadly had not returned. He had written Venna twice—polite, cynical letters, in which he assured her he would not return to the city until she was pleasantly located elsewhere for the summer. Would she inform him of her absence.

It seemed to Venna her whole life had collapsed. She saw nothing ahead of her but a sham existence, constantly scheming to hide the reality of her empty existence from her aunt and others. The fear of gossip among her friends worried her equally as much as the desire not to pain her aunt. Each day she sat in her room, thinking and perplexing herself with the thought of her future. Where could she go in the summer, alone—without society asking questions?

Oh, how she longed for Daddy, and the old times of freedom and light-heartedness. Every night she cried herself to sleep with Daddy upon her lips.

But there came no answer. Only a blank silence, bringing the reality of death's destruction to all hope and love. Some nights Venna couldn't sleep. She would lie with eyes wide open, praying God that she might die, too. But her prayer was a vague murmuring and God seemed very far off.

How she longed for some vital religion! The uncertain teachings of her childhood and girlhood did not help her in her despondency. She always had cherished the thought that her mother's spirit hovered near to her—there had been times when she felt her presence. Why did she not have that consolation now? She found no answer. She only knew that within her troubled heart, faith was at a very low ebb.

Today was a little harder than usual. A dull heavy atmosphere without did not tend to cheer. "If only the sun would shine! Anything, anything to lift this morbid, overpowering depression!"

As if in answer to her heart's cry, a cheery voice called outside her door,

"Venna! Venna! Let me in! I couldn't wait for you to come down. Open the door, dear, quick?"

Venna started with sudden heart-beating. Anna Halloway! Her school chum of happy days! Bright, joyous Anna!

One moment and the door was opened and Venna found herself sobbing hysterically in her friend's arms.

In surprise Anna hugged her close, and caressed her curls.

"Why, Venna dear, what is the matter? I expected to find my little bride all smiles. Oh, it's so good to see you after two long years. But not like this! What on earth troubles you?"

Venna did not immediately answer, but after Anna had calmed her with loving assurances, she said with a tired little smile, "O Anna, I've been so lonely. I believe God sent you right to me, you dear, cheerful thing! So much has happened to me since you went West."

"Tell me all about it," said Anna, still encircling her arms around Venna, as they sat down upon the couch.

So Venna, hungry for sympathy, laid bare her heart, as she never thought it possible for her to do.

Anna drew from her everything, though at times the confidence came in broken, timid sentences.

"So you see, Anna, what a failure my life has been," she concluded piteously.

Anna laughed.

"You little goose! Your first trials have knocked you right down and out, haven't they? I appreciate your position, dear, but I'll have you all smiles again, very soon. You need a strong, vital faith, dearie— something to lift you right up and keep you there."

"Yes, I know I need faith. I really *long* for it. But where and how are we to get it these days? And you, Anna—you were always so skeptical about religion?"

"Yes, I know I was, but I'm not now. I learned Christian Science since I saw you, dear. Oh, it's just wonderful, Venna. It will lift you out of *anything*."

"Christian Science? I always thought that more visionary than anything else, Anna."

"You don't understand it, dear. Of course, you'll say I have had no trials yet. That's true, but I'm ready for them. I know just how to meet them."

Anna Halloway was round, rosy and radiant—one of that type of healthy, practical womanhood, that imparts a glow to other natures by its warmth and dynamic force. She could not fully appreciate a nature as refined and aspiring as Venna's. On the other hand, Venna's receptive mind drew in gladly the joy of Anna's nature, and her thirsty soul was for the time refreshed.

"In the first place, Venna dear, you must get those ugly thoughts about your husband right out of your mind. You must think well of him—give him your best thoughts, as we say. Then you'll influence him for good."

"But, Anna, how can I think well of him when he married me after such a past? That was unfair to me."

"And you married him without loving him. Weren't you unfair to him? You gave him next to nothing. Now, dear, I'm going to be terribly frank with you, but there is no other way to bring you to your normal senses. I don't suppose you realize that you have led a very selfish life? Now don't feel hurt, dear. *You* couldn't help it. You've been loved and flattered ever since you were born. You've never sacrificed anything for anyone outside of Venna Hastings or Venna Hadly, have you? Now, dear, you have an unselfish nature. *I* know that,—but you've never used it. You have just received, received, received. Now just change your position in the bank and be paying teller for awhile."

"I suppose," Venna said reflectively, "if I had gone on with my settlement work, it *would* have helped."

"It wouldn't at all," exclaimed Anna, decisively. "The way we society women take up settlement work doesn't require any particular sacrifice. It's a novelty, a pleasure, a sort of 'satisfy conscience' relaxation. What you need now is to get out of *yourself*. Make a real sacrifice for some one who needs it—for instance, your husband."

"You mean I should live with him?" asked Venna, in sudden consternation.

Anna was momentarily taken back by the strength of the opposition.

"I would," she answered, seriously. "In your place, I would say to myself, 'He cheated me, I cheated him. That's equal. Now we'll make the best of life and help one another.' You know, Venna dear, the average man is no better than Hadly. It wasn't *his* fault that you were brought up with your eyes shut, was it? Why hate him any more than any one else? Be fair, Venna. He has a *right* to be well thought of in other respects."

Venna shook her head sadly.

"Yes, I sinned when I married without love. I see that now. But I never could love a man who looks upon his past impurity as a matter of course. So if I never could love him, where is the logic in remaining his wife?"

"Couldn't you pity him enough to let love creep in?" urged Anna.

"One can't love to order," returned Venna sadly.

"Well, if you can't, you can't," concluded Anna, giving up a hopeless case. "But at least, you won't hate him and treat him with scorn."

"No, Anna, I see where I'm not much better in many respects. You've opened my eyes to my own injustice. I'll try not to hate him, and—yes, it has been all self. I see it now."

"It is always self with us girls until we are mothers. Venna, I never woke up myself until—O, can't you guess, Venna? I have a wonderful surprise for you!" And she hugged Venna impulsively.

"You don't mean," began Venna, disentangling herself.

"Yes, I do mean!" interrupted Anna. "I'm the happy mother of a bouncing girlie six months old! I kept it as a surprise. She's such a darling, Venna!"

"I'm so glad for you, Anna. It must be a wonderful happiness to be a mother," she added wistfully.

"There, dear! I'm going to show you how to mother the whole world! No sad thoughts now. I think only of cheerful things. I'll have you the same old bright dear in no time. You shall spend the whole summer with me—we are going for six months, to a quiet little country place because of baby—where the air is fine and I can give my whole attention to her. Why, I hate the servants to even touch her! I'll let *you* though, and won't she make you laugh again! You'll forget what sadness is. You will go with us, won't you, dear?"

"Oh, how I would love to! Indeed I will!" exclaimed Venna, brightening. "God is good after all. He always finds us a way."

"Of course He's good, Venna, and gives us all Good. It is only our foolish mortal minds that imagine evil."

Venna did not understand what Anna meant, but she thanked God in her heart for sending her friend and with her the sunshine.

CHAPTER VI.

Under the influence of spring, sunshine and flowers, our souls give birth to new thoughts, new ambitions.

The little village store in Ashfield was buzzing. It was mail-time and the good wife of the proprietor, the post-master and mayor—in other words, the wife of the chief all-round citizen, was sorting and pigeon-holing the mail.

Around the store waited a goodly representation of the neighborhood—long, lanky workmen; fat, prosperous home-dwellers who "worked in the city," dirty little urchins with sticky hands, and pretty young girls stylishly dressed.

Quite a congregation of "American mixed," but the buzzing gave an air of congeniality which lent the impression of true democracy so typified in a Jersey village.

One young girl with roguish blue eyes sauntered up to a thin, neatly dressed elderly man, who was watching the group with a friendly smile.

"Have yer called on the new people yet, Mr. Allworth? There's a dandy young lady in the bunch. Don't let Pastor Soffy get ahead of you. We want her in *our* Church."

Her tone was loud enough to attract attention, and the majority suspended their buzzing.

The Methodist minister answered in a clerical tone,

"My dear Miss Bessie, I would never strive for members for our Church. Call I certainly shall, but not with the intention of robbing Mr. Soffy."

"Oh, fudge!" exclaimed Bessie, laughing, "everyone knows you'll both scramble for them!"

At this there was a general laugh, at which Mr. Allworth colored furiously.

It was plain to be seen Bessie was a privileged character.

"Stop your joshing, Bessie!" exclaimed the wife of the post-master, proprietor, and mayor. "Here's a letter for the new people. You take it up the road to them, and that'll get you acquainted."

"Sure I will!" returned Bessie with enthusiasm. "Dandy! I'll prepare the way for you, Mr. Allworth, and see that they don't get any Presbyterian ideas ahead of time!"

Mr. Allworth smiled and nodded his head.

"Yer won't git those new people and don't yer fergit it!" piped up one dirty little bare-legged urchin, sidling up to Bessie. "I spent two hours helping them clear up the lawn. Gosh! They're darn swell, all righty! Gave me a fifty. What do yer think o' that? Fifty in two hours, eh, boss?"

"Boss" shoved the ten-year old aside kindly.

"Out o' the way, Bud! Let me get behind that counter, will you? Go home and tell your mother you need sewing up. What do you know about the new people?" he asked, eyeing Bud whimsically, while he delved into the sugar tin.

"Whole lot, all righty! I told 'em I pumped the organ in Mr. Soffy's church, and ast them would they like ter see me."

The buzzing had completely stopped and all hands were at attention.

"And they said?" asked Boss Holden.

Bud swelled with the importance of delivering town news.

"They ast me what kind o' Church it was. I says, 'Sure, the kind yer pray in. What d' yer think?'"

"Good boy!" laughed Boss Holden, "And then?"

"They just laughed as though they had no sense, and guessed their kind o' Church waren't in these parts. I up and ast them what kind o' Church they wanted and they said 'Scientific.'"

"Bud, that thar waren't right nohow," spoke up John, colored chauffeur to the two rich old maids on the hill. "I heard Pastor Soffy tell my missus they war "Christian Scientissus.""

"Christian Scientists!" exclaimed Mr. Allworth with dignified disapproval. "What next will come into our little town!"

"Well, I'm going to take the letter up anyway," declared Bessie. "Good-bye. I'll do my best for you, Mr. Allworth," and with this parting shot she was gone.

Up the hill walked Bessie, round, fair and rosy, with her laughing blue eyes vieing merriment with her dimpled cheeks.

Half way up the hill, she stopped at a large "homey" white house which stood about fifty feet back from the road. Its broad piazzas were simply furnished with chairs, tables, and plants, all arranged for convenience and comfort.

Bessie tripped up the few steps leading to the front door and rang the bell.

The object of her admiration, the young lady with the light brown curls, opened the door.

"Here's a letter for a Mrs. Hadly," said Bessie in her most friendly voice. "Will you please give it to her?"

"Thank you. *I* am Mrs. Hadly. Won't you come in?"

Venna thought she would like to talk to this pretty young country girl. Everything and everyone seemed so new and interesting—so different to what she had been accustomed to in fashionable summer resorts.

Bessie was ready to accept the invitation.

"Yes, I would like to come in and get acquainted," she said frankly.

As she followed Venna into the large, cool living room, she felt a little disappointed at the thought of this fascinating city girl being married.

"It'll spoil all the fun," she decided.

"Do sit down," said Venna kindly as she seated herself. "So you are one of the young ladies of the village? Do tell me a little about the life here. It is all so new to me and my friend, too."

"Your friend? The lady with the baby?" asked Bessie.

"Yes, we are going to live here together. Mr. and Mrs. Halloway, baby, and myself and maids, for six months."

"Oh, then you're just summer people," said Bessie, disappointed again.

"Yes, my home is in New York. But six months is a long, long time," she added, smiling. She was amused at the open, admiring gaze of her visitor.

"I guess you'll have enough of it before six months is out. City people don't care much for Ashfield—that is, unless they stay and get used to it."

"Is it so very unpleasant here then?" asked Venna.

"Mercy, no!" exclaimed Bessie, ready to defend her own home town. "It's a dandy place when you're right in with everything. The summer people always stay on the outside—just look on, yer know, and of course it's awful slow compared to city life, and just being on the outside makes it slower."

"Yes, I understand. To like country life, one must know everyone for miles around," remarked Venna.

"Exactly, I don't suppose you'll want to do that, though," Bessie returned with hesitation.

"Not quite—as we don't expect to stay. But I won't remain on the 'outside' while I'm here. This life will be too interesting to me to ignore it. Tell me, what is the most important diversion in Ashfield?"

"Going to Church, I guess—or, the movies over in Ellenville," replied Bessie.

Venna laughed.

"Which do you like best?" she asked.

"Oh, I like both. The Church has lots of fun, though—always something going on. Which Church do you think you will like?"

"I don't know. There are two, aren't there? How did there ever happen to be more than one in this little place?"

"It was just this way," explained Bessie, pleased to give village history: "At one time, there was only one, the Methodist. But some of the members quarreled with the minister and left to start a church of their own. Just for spite they built it right opposite to ours, and they became Presbyterians. Kind o' mean, wasn't it? Of course, that was long ago. Since then the people have become friendly and the ministers exchange calls, but when anyone new comes to town, they both scramble for a new member. Has Mr. Soffy called yet?"

"No, but I expect him this afternoon. He met Mr. Halloway and asked if he might call today."

"There! I knew it!" exclaimed Bessie. "He always gets there first. I guess anyway you'll like Mr. Soffy and his Church best. Most city people do."

"Why so?"

"Well, you see Mr. Allworth is a plain country minister—never been anything else. You'll find him helping his wife do the wash, or feeding the chickens, or gossiping at the store, when he ought to be out making calls. Mr. Soffy is a young man who has worked his way through college and knows a lot about the new ideas that take well. And somehow he's always there first, and gets the city folks."

"He must be quite an interesting young man," returned Venna, amused at the queer little village and its doings. "I suppose he feels very important and popular."

"Well, hardly either," returned Bessie. "He seems very humble, considering how smart he is. And popular? Most of the people, especially the men, don't like him at all. Some don't like the way the old ladies on the hill fuss over him. They call him a 'molly' for letting them. You know he lives with the two Miss Haskells, and they fairly dote on him. It's 'Soffy here' and 'Soffy there' until one does get rather tired of it. But *I* like him. I think it's jealousy that makes him disliked. You see people here don't take to those who know a lot more than themselves. Mr. Allworth takes more with the country people."

"It must be rather a hard position for Mr. Soffy," said Venna with ready sympathy. "It's very discouraging to fight against prejudice."

"It certainly is," agreed Bessie. "But I hope you'll come to *our* Church. We need a few up-to-date people to liven things up a bit."

"Well, my dear, I certainly will attend both Churches sometimes—then no one will feel hurt."

"Oh, thank you. That's a fair, square deal."

"Of course, I won't join any; but while I'm here, I'm sure I would enjoy a simple country church. I don't know about Mrs. Halloway, however, she is a Christian Scientist."

"Then you are not?" asked Bessie delighted, vaguely imagining Christian Scientists belonged to some queer species.

"No, not exactly," returned Venna quietly. "But Christian Science has many beautiful beliefs that help one to live a better life."

"Is that so?" asked Bessie curiously. "Sometime will you tell me all about it?"

"Mrs. Halloway can do that better than I can. I know she would like to. You must call again when she is in."

There was a pause in the conversation and Bessie decided it wouldn't do to stay too long the first time.

"I will call again, thank you," she replied, as she arose to go. "Thank you very much for saying you'll come to our church."

As Venna stood on the porch watching Bessie go up the hill, the warmth and glow of the beautiful May day seemed to thrill her whole being. The air was laden with the scent of apple-blossoms, and the fresh green of the trees and grass invited one to new thoughts and a new life.

When Bessie reached the top of the hill she turned and waved her hand. Venna waved back.

"How friendly and primitive it all is!" was Venna's pleased thought. "That bright, happy face—it seems it ought to be easy to live Christian Science here."

Certainly Anna Halloway had done wonders for Venna. Whether Christian Science or Anna's personal influence played the greater part in taking Venna out of her depths, it would be hard to determine. Both, however, played important parts. A few weeks had brought to Venna the determination to think only of happy things and service to others. She was learning the lesson of looking "up" and not "down," "out" and not "in," and to a nature so naturally bright as hers, it was not a very difficult task. Hadly did not annoy her at all. Since she came to Ashfield one week ago, she received a formal letter from him, stating his return to New York and asking her to write if she desired anything at his hands. Nothing could be more cooly polite.

"Poor Hadly! He certainly is acting his very best under the circumstances," she decided, and she gave him her "best thoughts," as Anna entreated her to do.

Just before Bessie came, she had been wondering what she could do in this little village to make more happiness for someone.

The whole six months in Anna's cheerful company would give her time to recover herself and lay plans for a useful future, but busy she must be wherever she was, or her despondency might return. Bessie's visit gave her a sudden happy thought. Why not interest herself in the girls of the village? The Church and the movies! Was that all they had?

She seated herself in a low wicker porch chair to read her letter from Aunt Emily.

"Detroit, Wednesday.
"Venna Dearest:

"Just a line to let you know Dr. Hansom and I are both well and enjoying our trip so very much. Detroit gave us a wonderful welcome. Somehow they found out we were here, and one of the Churches gave us a big dinner. I wish you could have heard him speak! He was so earnest and yet so witty at times! How proud I was of him! Dearie, how thankful we ought both to be that we have such excellent husbands and are so happy! How glad your dear father would be! I suppose your good Hadly commutes to Ashfield. Or is he too busy? You must find it much pleasure to be with Anna again, though I'm surprised you would choose a dead little country place. Don't you think it may be very monotonous for you? Surely you will find very few of your class there.

"Well, dearie, whatever makes you happy, of course, do. I suppose you are beginning to realize Hadly is all that is necessary for your happiness.

"Dr. Hansom has received so many earnest requests to preach in Western cities, that we may spend the entire summer touring and satisfying the demand for his preaching.

"In spite of all my new happiness, I miss you so, dearie. Do write constantly. Give my love to Anna and Hadly.

"I am anxious to see that precious baby. Perhaps one day there will be one more precious you can show me.

"By-bye, dear girlie.

"Your loving Aunt Emily."

As Venna finished the letter, her face saddened and she lost herself in thoughts of the past and what might have been. But she quickly drew herself together.

"This is not Christian Science!" she declared to herself. "Away with such thoughts and enter sunshine, flowers, spring-time!"

"Good afternoon," said a pleasant, full-toned man's voice, and Venna looked up to see Mr. Soffy enter her gate. She knew him because Halloway had pointed him out as one of the main objects of interest.

"Good afternoon," she returned, rising and taking in his pleasant personality at a glance.

Mr. Soffy was medium height, rather fleshy, with dark, wavy hair above a broad, large-featured face, from which looked out dreamy, dark eyes. His smile was particularly frank and broad, showing white, even teeth between full, sensuous lips.

A few pleasantries were exchanged as they entered the house and the living room.

"It is a great pleasure for me to meet you," began Mr. Soffy, taking in with delight the beauty and brightness of this new comer. "Every little while, some city people will wander out here and it is so refreshing to meet them."

"How strange!" said Venna, smiling. "I find the country people so refreshing. Such a bright, rosy, blue-eyed girl has just called. She seemed to bring a breath of spring with her."

"Yes? Oh, I've no doubt that was Bessie, a winsome Methodist girl. Pretty, isn't she? All the country boys are wild over her, but she declares she'll marry a city chap or none."

"She might do better right here," said Venna seriously.

"Yes, that's very true. I'm a city man myself, and I think the men of the simple life compare very favorably with the men of the city's whirl. But if you like country people, you'll meet all your heart can desire. As soon as they know you've settled, and Bessie will quickly report—all the ladies in the village will call, so prepare for a siege!"

"Will they?" asked Venna, smiling. "Mrs. Halloway and I must be prepared."

"No preparation necessary," replied Mr. Soffy, laughing. "They would rather take you unaware, and if anyone calls when you're washing, they would like nothing better than to come in the back way, seating themselves in the kitchen with a 'Never mind, my dear, go right on. We can get just as well acquainted, and you getting your work done.'"

Venna laughed with real amusement.

"Are they really so informal?"

"Yes, indeed; Primitive with a capital P. But I don't suppose you ever do such a thing as wash?"

"I must confess my ignorance in that line," returned Venna.

Mr. Soffy smiled understandingly. "I hope you will come out to our little Church sometimes?"

"Yes, I told Bessie I would divide my attentions between the two Churches."

"You have no choice then between the Methodist and the Presbyterian?"

"Hardly; I can't honestly say I have found any Church to satisfy me yet. Every denomination has so many inconsistencies. I love my Bible, and it doesn't seem to me that any of you fully follow Christ's teachings."

"To be frank with you," returned Mr. Soffy, contracting his brows thoughtfully, "I don't think any of us do. The Churches have accumulated the errors of ages. I wish personally we could throw off a lot of waste material. But the people have to be dealt with gradually. It's like operating on a diseased body. One part must be cut at a time or the patient would lose his life from shock."

"I can't agree with you," returned Venna earnestly. "Why should you preach error and intensify the disease?"

"Well—no—maybe not," returned Mr. Soffy with hesitation. "I never thought of it in just that light. It's very hard to know how to handle a congregation of church-goers today. They are full of prejudice, 'mother told me so' doctrines, and unless something new is startlingly attractive, out goes the preacher if he dares to introduce it. What would *you* do?" he asked with a look of open admiration.

Venna answered without hesitation.

"What would *I* do? If I were a preacher, I would study and pray hard to find the truth. And whatever I found, I would preach to my people, regardless of anyone's opinions or the keeping of my position. *You* regard truth as a knife that cuts away diseased parts one at a time. So you use it carefully. *I* regard truth as a healing stream that should flow freely at all times to heal the diseases of our minds."

Mr. Soffy's dark eyes reflected her enthusiasm.

"Wonderfully said!" he exclaimed. "If I had a few like you in my church, I would have the courage to do as you say."

"Courage comes from God, Mr. Soffy, not from man," returned Venna softly.

There was a moment's silence in which Mr. Soffy eyed Venna keenly as if to read her very soul.

"Are you a Christian Scientist?" he asked.

"Not exactly," replied Venna. "Mrs. Halloway is trying to make me one. I live by many of their principles. There is so much beauty in some of their ideas. But I must believe in the Personality of God. I can't see how they do away with it. When Stephen was being stoned to death, the heavens opened before him, and he saw the Christ sitting on the right hand of God. Now, if we believe in the inspiration of the Bible, how can we accept this vision without the belief in God's personality? There are many more verses in scripture which declare that truth also. I must believe all the Bible or none. There is no logic in accepting just those parts that we desire to accept. That is why all the Churches differ. They don't really accept the Bible as God's word. They often say they do, but if they really did, beliefs would be founded on the fullness of its teachings and not on man's opinions. Not only this, but when I have been in my greatest sorrows, I have longed for a personal God who understands. Religion wouldn't mean anything to me without the Personality of a Divine Father."

"I think you'd better take my pulpit, Mrs. Hadly," said Mr. Soffy smiling. "You have more decision of thought than myself."

"Oh, don't say that!" replied Venna. "I don't want to give the impression of sureness. Indeed, a few points I have decided, but the greater truths I am still seeking and praying for. I am very much at sea."

"Then keep on praying and remember the verse in the Bible you are so sure is inspired. 'If any of you lack wisdom, let him ask of God, that giveth to all men liberally, and upbraideth not; and it shall be given him.'"

Venna's eyes shone. "How often I have repeated that verse! Yes, I believe it, too. I am waiting for greater light on many things. I'm sure God will give it."

"But you must let go of prejudice to be in a condition to receive new ideas," returned Mr. Soffy. "I have thrown tradition to the winds, and find it easy to broaden out, but my congregation would be more than astounded if I told them all my ideas."

"I hope you will tell me many of them, Mr. Soffy. I like to hear new thoughts, but I always sift them well before I give them precedence over the old."

"Indeed, it will be a pleasure to discuss with a mind like yours," returned he with his broadest smile. "I hope you will permit me to call often. I must go now, however, for I promised to address the woman's club this afternoon. Perhaps next time I come, it will be in the evening, that I might meet Mr. Hadly, too. He commutes with Mr. Halloway?"

Venna dropped her eyes and colored noticeably.

"No, Mr. Hadly will not be in Ashfield—for a time. He is very busy in the city."

Mr. Soffy was quick to detect her confusion, but, making no further remark concerning her husband, he said good-bye with a firm pressure of her hand in his.

"Remember, Mrs. Hadly, I am always at your service. Do not hesitate to call upon me."

After he had gone, Venna attempted to read without success. The words before her seemed meaningless. Against her will she was comparing Hadly and this young minister. The comparison was unfavorable to her husband.

"What a personality!" she said to herself, thinking of the young minister and letting her imagination build a character for him that was exceptional. "Why did not my life bring me to a man like him when I was free? Yet probably I could never have loved him. I can't really imagine myself being in love and why?"

But her self analysis always ended in a question, and was left to future answering.

Venna was an enigma to herself to be solved only by truths gained by experience.

CHAPTER VII.

To the so-called "broad thinker" of today, Satan comes as "an angel of light."

Mr. Allworth did not call on Mrs. Hadly and Mrs. Halloway. He had his own very unfavorable opinion of Christian Scientists and he didn't think it his duty to encourage such people to come to his church and perhaps introduce their pernicious doctrines among his flock. It was best "to leave well enough alone," he decided in his good old-fashioned way.

But Mr. Soffy called many times. Mr. and Mrs. Halloway liked him immensely. Both found him an excellent listener, and one who made concessions to their ideas in a most pleasing manner. Mr. Halloway was not over enthusiastic over Christian Science, but as his wife was such a devout believer, he fell in line gracefully, and decided it was about as near the truth as any other creed. He was a large, good-natured Englishman, brought up in the Episcopal Church in America, which is so spiritless and conventional that thousands like himself constantly drift away, not because of any dislike or hatred of the Church but from sheer indifference to the religious apathy and lifeless conditions. By contrast the positive convictions and enthusiasm in his wife's religion was, to say the least, attractive. So he tried to enter into her thoughts as far as his big, practical manhood would allow. But there were times when argument would evolve. And more often than not, it would happen so when Mr. Soffy called. Then it was that the minister showed to greatest advantage. With Mr. Halloway, Anna and Venna before him, he had three intelligent minds, all in reality differing considerably. With tact, he handled each one. Offending none, he almost proved that all were right, and left the impression that he was both tactful and broad-minded.

Mr. and Mrs. Halloway declared him "splendid," "an exceptional young man."

Venna acquiesced mildly enough, but with every meeting, her admiration for him increased.

Very often he would "just step in for a few moments" in the afternoon when he knew he would likely find her alone. These were the times Venna enjoyed the most. They would have such heart-to-heart talks upon all subjects. And there was also a great deal of planning to do concerning the affairs of the little church. Venna found herself soon a regular attendant and was early persuaded to take a Sunday School class for the summer.

"We need you so badly," Mr. Soffy had pleaded, and that was enough for Venna's ready sympathy. So she undertook a class of ten year old boys— laughing, rollicking country lads who had the name of being the worst class in the school. Venna soon learned to manage them and had each one "adoring" her before the month was past. "Bud" was her favorite, and every day he made his appearance with a bunch of flowers and a few remarks containing the latest news of Ashfield.

Then her idea of being interested in the young girls materialized into a recreation club, which brought joy to the hearts of the girls and considerable planning to the mind of Venna. Picnics, entertainments for the church, club meetings, etc., were always on the programme, and the life of the Ashfield lassie was a happier affair since Mrs. Hadly entered town. Of course, there were some people who criticized.

"I'm not so sure," remarked Miss Harriet Haskell, "but that the girls are giving less thought to Mission study."

"I fear that it is sadly true," replied her sister Mary dubiously. "These city people will turn our girls' heads with their frivolous ideas. Does it not occur to you, Harriet, that it is rather queer that Mr. Hadly is too busy to come to Ashfield?"

"I should say so, indeed," replied Harriet Haskell, her thin lips tightening in strong disapproval. "Perhaps she's a divorced woman. Nothin' would surprise me now-a-days. We've had some strange 'goin's on' in this town sometimes. We'd better keep our eyes open, I'm thinkin'."

"That we had," returned sister Mary in her mild but sure tone. "Those curls are certainly coquettish. I don't like the arrangement of them. They're not the Lord's doin', I'm persuaded of that."

"The Lord never put it into the heart of any married woman to try to fascinate a young minister," returned Harriet more sharply. "If these calls don't lessen a bit, I'm going to speak to Mr. Soffy myself. Indeed he's too young and good to understand scheming women. And even if she were innocent, and very little hope I have of that, the talk is all over town and you know it doesn't take much to start gossip here. People won't mind their business. It's strange to me how evil-minded every one is."

"The world is very sinful, that's true," returned mild Mary piously. "We must try and counteract the influence of all these frivolous ideas Mrs. Hadly is introducing. I was told she had all the young people dancing at her house last night."

"I know she did. She can't deny it. Mr. Soffy was there, too, and didn't disapprove. Thank heaven he refused to dance himself. Really, we can expect anything now-a-days. I spoke to him this morning about it, and he said, 'Really, Miss Harriet, you can't expect young people to think of religion all the time. Let them dance and have a good time, as long as they're in good company.'"

"He said that?" asked Miss Mary in horrified disapproval. "Why only a month ago, I heard him tell a young lady dancing was an insidious sin."

"Yes, my dear," replied Miss Harriet, "but he's talking through Mrs. Hadly now. Influence is everything, you know. He is so good, and it is our bounden duty to protect him. We must be 'wise as serpents and harmless as doves.' Just watch out and learn all you can and maybe we can stay the evil. Thank Goodness, she goes in a few months."

And so Venna was the subject of discussion in more homes than one. She didn't return calls or mix in with the pleasure of the older people. She pleaded lack of time and a desire to make the young people happy. But this excuse was received with strong doubt.

The wise heads got close together with a significant "Maybe!" and then an offended "Does she think Ashfield isn't good enough without her improvin'?"

Venna's ideas of country life and its sentiments were within the range of simple living, honest goodwill, and glorious inspirations from green hills and wild flowers. She interpreted it through her own nature and found it most attractive.

Seeing only the surface of this simple life in Ashfield naturally confirmed her ideas, and she found great happiness in this altogether new existence.

But the undercurrent in human nature surged here as elsewhere, and would eventually rise to the surface to play havoc in Venna's life.

Meanwhile Venna's ten girls were happy and worshipful in Venna's presence. The village wondered that the mothers seemed pleased, too. Bessie was a constant visitor with the city people and sharp as she was to detect village sentiment, she carefully kept all rumors from Venna, and gave her opinion airily in the store as to what "old fogies wished young people to be."

Ashfield was really enjoying itself. Unless you have lived in a little place like that, you cannot appreciate the pleasure the people derive from "some one new to talk about."

It was a wonderful June afternoon when Mr. Soffy sauntered in at the little white gate, and stood for a moment contemplating the roses arranged artistically in large jardinieres on the porch. Their fragrance was heavy and filled the air as one approached. Of course, Venna's hand had arranged them. Everything worth while in this home spoke of Venna. So thought Mr. Soffy. His admiration for her had developed into a strong passion. Two months ago Ashfield had seemed a monotonous hole. Now it was a rose garden, filled with love's anticipations. Everytime he left that rose garden, he knew it was but to come again into the presence of this exceptional woman. What if she were married? She was unhappy and had never known what love really meant. Why should a woman go through life unloved? Such "old fogy" ideas belonged to "Miss Mary" and "Miss Harriet" but not to broad-minded, up-to-date people. Of course, he must think of his church people. They were too far behind the times to appreciate any of nature's laws, so he must be careful. If he could win her love, it must be under cover, without any outside criticism to disturb their mutual happiness.

He could plainly see how they could live ideally. Their minds were seemingly an open book to one another, and her beauty would lead any man to do his best for her, and so the Rev. Mr. Soffy, with his broad, new way of thinking, was planning and hoping to make Venna the greatest love of his life. Other loves had been his, but this was to be the one supreme and lasting one, even though marriage by law was impossible. After all, an outward marriage was simply form. The true marriage was the union of two hearts. So reasoned Mr. Soffy and secretly justified himself.

While his thoughts and the fragrance of roses were filling him with dreamy satisfaction, Venna opened the door with baby Halloway in her arms.

As she stood in the open door-way she made a sweet picture of motherhood.

Conscience spoke:

"The crowning glory to woman is motherhood."

Passion answered:

"You are doing this woman no harm. She wouldn't be a mother anyway."

Conscience retreated.

"I'm so glad to see you, Mr. Soffy. Mr. and Mrs. Halloway have gone to the city and won't be home until to-morrow. I volunteered to take care of baby, so I can't be with the girls to rehearse this afternoon. Would you mind stepping into the hall and telling them to go over their parts alone. I want to-night to be a glorious success. Come in a moment, won't you?"

"Your wonderful violin makes everything a success," he returned, entering the house, and holding out his arms to the baby in a most inviting manner.

Little Anna smiled and stretched out her wee baby hands in response. Taking her in his arms, he began to talk to her in true baby fashion while Venna looked on pleased.

"You ought to be married, Mr. Soffy, and have a family of your own. You like children, don't you?"

"Yes. They know how to love without criticising. It's some satisfaction to win hearts like they possess."

"Don't you like to be criticised?"

"Not particularly. The critic seldom knows the truth about the one he criticises. For instance," he said smiling down at her, "you're not the only one who tells me I ought to be married. If I could have the right woman, I would marry to-morrow. But as I cannot, I will never marry."

A passionate look of admiration accompanied his words. There was no mistaking the meaning of it.

With the sudden shock of this revelation, Venna's whole being tingled with shame. She dropped her eyes in confusion, but suddenly raised them again in anger.

What could she say? He had not said anything that she could resent.

For a moment they looked into one another's eyes in silence, his gaze pleading with her anger more eloquently than words could have done. Gradually her look softened and she held out her arms for Anna.

"It is time for me to bathe baby," she said as naturally as she could. "You will tell the girls?"

Mr. Soffy knew this was meant for him to go.

"Don't disappoint to-night."

"Oh, no—Stella will be through with her work then and will take Anna."

For a moment he stood irresolute. Should he speak of his love now? They were alone. But that look of anger—what did she mean by it? Perhaps she was not yet ready to accept broad ideas of love. No, he must not be rash. He would bide his time—though his passion longed to declare itself. So with a quick decision to go carefully for this great treasure, he held out his hand in his usual cheery way.

"Good-bye then. I won't detain you from your motherly duties. I'll look forward to seeing you to-night."

Without another word he was gone, and Venna found herself alone.

Impulsively she hugged and kissed baby Anna, and so gave vent to her odd mixture of emotions.

"O baby girl!" she murmured. "If only you were my own sweet babe, and I had to mother you morn, noon and night, then, dearie, nothing so awful could ever have happened?"

Anna gurgled for reply and cuddled comfortably against Venna's cheek, stretching out baby hands to play with the attractive curls.

Was he really in love with her or did she imagine it? What a fine man he was! How she admired him! He was such a good friend—why couldn't he remain so? No, she hadn't encouraged him to love her. She never dreamed of anything so dishonorable. But they were congenial. She might have known. In this lonely little place, it was natural for him to fall into channels of feeling without his own consent even. No, she wouldn't be angry—he couldn't help it.

She must pity him and respect his hopeless love. Of course, if he had spoken, it would be different. But he was too honorable for that. He couldn't help having eyes that expressed every feeling he possessed. His eyes were indeed eloquent. How strange that Fate threw them together at this impossible time.

If she had been free—who knows? She might have learned to love him.

These musings were suddenly interrupted by a loud bang of the kitchen door, and Stella's voice raised in sharp protest.

"If you don't learn to come in quietly, you'll stay out, young man."

Venna smiled. She knew this was Bud, who had free access at all times, much to Stella's disapproval.

There was a fairly well-controlled knock, and at Venna's "Come in" Bud entered on tip-toe.

He was always "washed up," with the shoes that Venna had given him well "shined," when he called on this wonderful lady of his dreams.

"Thot I'd step in an' give yer the news," he said, seating himself familiarly.

"Yes, Bud dear, but be quick for baby is waiting for her bath and I have several things to fix for the wonderful entertainment to-night. You're going to be there?"

"You bet! But, Missus Hadly, I've got spicy news. There's mermaids in town!"

"Mermaids!" laughed Venna. "What on earth do you mean, Bud?"

Bud colored.

"I may ha' got the name some twisted, but they're here, jes the samey. They're pretty bad 'uns, too, so everyone says."

"You'll have to find out the real name, Bud, before you can frighten me."

"There goes Bessie. I'll call her in," and, suiting his action to his words, he ran to the door and hailed Bessie.

Bessie entered the house, her rosy face all smiles.

"Say, Bess," said Bud confidently, "I've got the swell news jes' a bit twisted. What's the name o' those guys jes' come in, that everyone's slammin'?"

"Oh, you mean those two Mormon preachers. Just think, Mrs. Hadly, there are two young men walking through the country here without any money, just like tramps and calling themselves preachers for Christ. They say they are awful people and run away West with all the pretty girls they can find. Did you ever hear of them?"

Venna's eyes brightened with interest.

"Oh, yes, I've heard of them. I don't believe they are as bad as they're made out to be."

Venna's mind traveled quickly back to that memorable night on Broadway and the young Mormon's face came vividly to her recollection.

"Don't yer think they're not!" bursted in Bud excitedly. "They're bin astin' everyone in town ter sleep in their barns 'cause they hev no money. Every one's skiddooed 'em alrighty. Better look out, Bess! You're darn pretty, yer know!"

Venna laughed. "They wouldn't hurt anyone, Bud. That's my opinion."

"Is it?" asked Bessie puzzled.

"There they come now," exclaimed Bud, excitedly running to the window. "Shall I open the door and kick 'em out?" he asked, swelling with importance.

"You'll just be a good boy and say nothing. I'll open my door myself," she returned smiling, as she went into the hall, with baby Anna still clinging to her curls.

Bud looked after her with fearful admiration.

"Gosh! Bess! Ain't she brave? We'll stay quiet like, but won't budge till they git out. We may be needed," he said significantly.

As Venna opened the door, two tired looking young men respectfully lifted their hats.

The younger one, deathly pale, held the arm of the older one who spoke.

"Madam, we are Mormon missionaries, traveling without purse or scrip to preach the gospel of Christ. My companion here is ill from fatigue. If you will kindly permit us to sleep in your barn, we will be grateful."

Venna gazed at the speaker with a sudden thrill of recognition and pleasure. Before her stood the young preacher of Broadway. He was older and more manly, but there was no mistaking the earnest face with its deep-set gray eyes.

"Let us forget the barn. Come in, and we'll see what I can offer you," she said cordially.

As she led them into the living room, the smile of relief on the younger man's face touched Venna.

"Sit down—no, not there—take these comfortable chairs," she said, indicating two large cushioned armchairs which the weary travelers accepted gratefully.

Bessie looked down and nervously toyed with the lace of her pretty blue dress. Bud fixed his suspicious and defiant eyes upon the intruders, shifting his gaze from one to the other like a watchful bull-dog.

The elder man laughed.

"My lad, you don't look friendly. Come, shake hands. We're harmless."

Bud's hand was not forthcoming. He arose in the full dignity of his ten years, fearless and determined.

"I know yer, if she don't. What yer comin' here fer? Yer better look out! Spose yer think there's no men folks here ter lick yer, eh? Well, one's a' coming wi' the next train alrighty!"

The two young men smiled through their weariness.

"I'm glad, madam, you don't share his sentiments," said the younger.

"You must not mind Bud," Venna returned laughing. "He is my chief protector. Now, Bud, if I told you I knew one of these young men and respected him greatly, what would you do?"

Bud's eyes grew round with wonder and Bessie looked up in astonishment.

The young men watched Venna keenly, surprised at this method of subduing Bud.

Bud's voice was rather reluctantly hesitating.

"Spose, Missus Hadly, if they was yer friends they'd ha' ter be alrighty!"

Bessie rose rather hurriedly, anxious not to offend her new friend, but more anxious to feel sure she was out of danger.

"I'll have to hurry on to rehearsal now. I'll see you to-night," and with a timid glance at the two intruders she said a hurried good-bye and was gone.

"Now Bud, dear, you run on, too," said Venna kindly. "I want to talk to my friends alone awhile—friends—you understand. Bud? Don't forget—*friends*."

Bud's round face rippled into a broad grin.

"Well, I'll be jiggered! Some news I'll give 'em back alrighty. An' here I've bin slammin' wi' the rest o' em! Sorry, right sure I am. Shake!"

And Bud put forth both hands heartily. The young men pressed the little hands hard.

"We'll be good friends. Bud—you always go on defending the ladies!"

"You bet! When they 'semble her!"

The beloved "her" stooped over to kiss him good-bye.

"On your way out. Bud, tell Stella I said you were to have three big sugar cookies. Also ask Stella to take baby for awhile."

"Golly! Thanks!" And Bud disappeared.

When Stella had taken baby, Venna seated herself opposite the young men and regarded them seriously.

"They say terrible things about you, don't they? You don't look that kind."

"Do you believe them?" asked the older one, fixing his earnest gaze upon her unflinchingly.

"No. I might have though, if I hadn't met you before. Do you remember one night on Broadway, over two years ago, when you were preaching, a girl stepped up and played the violin for you?"

"Indeed, yes," he replied, quickly. "And you?"

"I was that girl. Your earnestness that night compelled me to believe in your sincerity. I read all your interesting tracts, and wished several times that I could see you again and talk them over."

The missionary gave a big sigh.

"My! You can't possibly realize what a joy it is to meet someone at last who really wants to hear our message. It is like an oasis in a desert. God surely led us here."

"I believe He did," returned Venna, smiling. "But we won't talk now. I have a spare room I wish you to have until you are quite rested for another trip. If you will retire now and wash up a bit, I will get my maid to prepare you a little lunch. You're hungry?"

"We've eaten nothing for two days," said the younger one, trying to smile but looking rather sad at the effort.

"How dreadful!" exclaimed Venna, horrified. "Come, I will show you your room, and hurry down again, for you both look pale from hunger."

"We can never thank you enough for this. Miss."

"Mrs. Hadly is my name," said Venna with simple dignity. "And yours?" she asked as they followed her upstairs.

"My name is Hallock. My companion is Brother Johnson," returned the older one.

Venna led them to the open door of a large airy room, the guest room, furnished daintily in blue and white.

The young men peered in. "Surely not for us?" said the younger. "We wouldn't like to disturb such daintiness."

"Go right in and make yourself at home. Daintiness is always refreshing when one is tired. I will give you just ten minutes to reappear!" and with her most winning smile, she left them.

The two young men stood for a moment looking at one another.

"Some one always materializes to save us on the last stretch," remarked the younger in a tired voice.

"Come brace up, old boy. You'll feel better when you have a rest. She's wonderful, isn't she?"

"Yes, God is good to send us here. I certainly wouldn't have lasted another day."

Meantime Venna surprised Stella into consternation.

"Quick, Stella! Something—anything to eat. Just set the table with anything. Put baby in the chair. They're just about starved. My heart just aches for them."

"Who's starved, ma'am? Have they come home early and nothing to eat in the city—that's no sense, sure," returned Stella, bustling about nervously.

"No, no, Stella. They haven't come home yet. It's two young men preaching throughout this wicked country of ours—just think, Stella! Preaching! Trying to save souls, and they're practically starving. They'll be down in a few minutes and we'll feed them well!"

Crash went a plate! Venna turned to see Stella standing, a picture of sudden fear, pale as death.

"You—don't—mean—the Mormons—are in—this house?" she gasped.

"Why, Stella! What on earth has frightened you. Of course, I do."

"O ma'am, last night at the party, everybody's man or maid was informed about those awful men. Aren't you afraid? I'll never sleep under the same roof with them, ma'am, that I won't. What will Mrs. Halloway say?"

"Look here, Stella, I'll have to tell you what I told Bud. I know one of these men. It's all talk. They're awfully good. Now hasten to prepare for my *friends*."

Stella's color gradually returned. "Are you sure, ma'am? Of course, if you've known them before I won't listen to others—but it's awful strange business, ma'am, it is—yes, I'm not glad they're here. Won't they go, ma'am?"

"Not if I wish them to stay!" replied Venna with dignity.

Stella always knew what that tone meant and in silence set the table lavishly. However, within her, there were throbbings of her poor heart that she had never experienced before and strange sensations of unusual chills crept up and down her being.

"It may be all right, but"—and she shook her head doubtfully.

Meanwhile Bud delightedly made his way to the store. There were a few villagers buying anything from a two-cent stamp to a bag of chicken feed. Boss Holden was not rushed. Afternoon buyers were always leisurely. Now was Bud's opportunity. He entered the store noisily.

"What d'yer think?" he asked, with both hands thrust deep into his pockets.

"Too warm to think, Bud," replied Boss Holden, smiling.

"Not w'en yer correctin' error," returned Bud, with serious importance, looking from one to the other.

"Error? That's some word for you. Bud! What's up now? You're as good as a 'Daily.' Why don't you print yourself black and white?" said Holden, with a laugh.

"Cause the print 'ud stick and news is allus changing. Yer know the talk about the mer—Mormon fellers? Well, every one's twisted. They're alrighty, I tell you."

Mr. Allworth contracted his Methodist brows into a slow frown.

"Who's been deceiving you, my lad? The Mormons themselves maybe? Stay clear of them. They'll do you no good."

"It's not themselves," returned Bud quickly. "It's Mrs. Hadly. She ses they're her *friends*. They're going ter stay wi' her. So they're alrighty, eh? What yer say ter thet?"

"Mrs. Hadly's friends!" exclaimed Miss Harriet Haskell, dropping her sugar to the floor in a general spill.

"I said it!" returned Bud decidedly. "An' the hull town's bin slammin' her *friends*. Nasty, mean, eh?"

Mr. Allworth never cared much for Miss Harriet, but this was a trying moment when all Christian hearts should be united. He looked at the old lady beseechingly.

"What can we do about this. Miss Harriet? Their evil influence will even spread to the children!"

"Isn't it awful?" came in almost frightened response. "Suppose—suppose we unite the forces of our churches to stay this evil. It's really a menace!"

"Now I see why Mrs. Hadly loved girls. I always had my suspicions of her. And now! Oh, it's too awful to think of!"

There were various degrees of fear expressed on the faces of the listeners.

Bud's cheeks were puffing out with fiery redness. At last he exploded.

"If anyone's goin' ter slam Missus Hadly, I'll make it hot fer them!"

"Shame o' yer. Bud! I'll tell yer mother o' yer impudence!" spoke up one shrewd-eyed little widow who received scraps from Miss Haskell's larder.

"I'm not ashamed! You bet, I'm not," defiantly returned Bud. "She's the best 'un in this mean old scrap-heap, where a feller can't lose a button 'thout every one a' knowing it!"

"Damn it, you're right. Bud!" exclaimed Boss Holden, bringing his fist down suddenly upon the counter. "Mrs. Hadly's one fine little woman. She shan't be talked over in my store!"

Mr. All worth gasped.

Miss Harriet paled.

The on-lookers smiled.

This was the limit of endurance.

"My dear man," said Allworth on recovering, "if you can't join a church, at least be respectful."

"And keep your swearing for other company, please!" added Miss Harriet sharply. "Come, Mr. Allworth, let us leave this place and talk the matter over like Christians!"

Exeunt the leaders of the flock.

Boss Holden drew a deep breath and laughed.

Bud jumped up on the counter and slapped Holden's arm.

"Bully! Boss! Yer good stuff!"

"So are you, Bud. Here!" and Holden's big hand transferred some bright alluring gum drops to the little outstretched, "ever-ready" one.

"To hell with their gossip!" exclaimed Boss to the onlookers.

"Them's my sentiments, too!" added Bud joyously.

While Bud was playing the hero at Holden's store, Bessie was doing her part with the girls. However, she was fortunate in finding no opposition.

"If they're Mrs. Hadly's friends, they'll pass," all agreed.

"What are they like? Are they good-looking? Are they pious?" were the questions thrown at Bessie with girlish impatience.

"They're just ordinary men, rather pale and tired, of course. Don't suppose they'll come out to-night. We'll all drop in to see Mrs. Hadly to-morrow, accidentally, you know. What fun! Let's plan to scare the 'fogies' in town!"

And instead of rehearsing, the girls planned.

CHAPTER VIII.

If Dame Gossip enjoyed revelling in the good instead of the evil, what universal joy her tongue would give!

Venna was late to her entertainment. Anna Halloway had telephoned that business would delay them in New York for several days. Would Venna mind if she were alone that long? If so, Anna told her to come in with Stella and the baby.

Venna answered that she would rather stay in Ashfield, and told Anna not to worry about her. Everything was all right and baby fine. She did not say anything about her new visitors—it wouldn't be easy to explain over the phone. She knew Anna would have done the same thing.

Brother Johnson and Brother Hallock (Venna thought it was odd but rather nice for them to call one another "Brother") certainly had enjoyed the meal Venna prepared. She enjoyed watching their delight with everything. The mother in her was touched.

"Think of them having no one to take care of their meals, and just eating anything they chance to get!"

After they had joyfully feasted, Venna excused herself and hurried her duties through as quickly as possible. Nevertheless she was late. The girls were all a trifle excited when she arrived, but the curtain soon went up, and the unusually large audience was quiet.

The play was a great success and Venna never played her violin more wonderfully. Mr. Soffy sat in a front seat and Venna felt his dark eyes watching her constantly. His admiration seemed to stimulate her to do her best. But withal the atmosphere of the evening was disquieting. So much whispering in the audience, so many furtive looks cast upon her.

What was unusual? Venna felt a strangeness but couldn't explain it.

After the entertainment was over, she did not come forward as usual, but busied herself with the girls clearing things up, and did not notice their suppressed giggles.

Mr. Soffy had lingered behind to escort Venna home. He always found an excuse for this, if she were alone. Miss Harriet and Miss Mary lingered, too, with the intention of not leaving him in danger, but he thwarted their good intentions with a bland smile.

"Now, don't you bother waiting for me. Miss Mary," he said in his pleasantest tone. "I wish to consult Mrs. Hadly regarding the picnic, and seeing her now will save me a call, you know."

"Oh, very well!" returned Miss Mary. "We will be going on then."

And as they were "going on" Miss Mary's head nodded with satisfaction. "The dear boy! You see, Harriet, my advice has been timely. He's trying to cut down his calls!"

"About time!" replied Miss Harriet sharply. "But it's her fault—not his!"

At this moment Mrs. Hadly found herself hurriedly kissed by her girls.

"Quick, girls! They'll be up the hill before we catch them," exclaimed Bessie impatiently. The girls all laughed.

"What on earth are you up to?" asked Venna, smiling.

"We'll tell you later—some good joke!" exclaimed Bessie, as she and her companion rushed out of the hall, throwing kisses back to her as they went.

"Be careful!" she called after them.

Alone with Mr. Soffy, Venna felt unusually embarrassed. There was a selfish pleasure in knowing he loved her, but the knowledge was disquieting to her conscience. She should be sorry, not glad. How weak she was in her loneliness!

The world seemed all wrong to her to-night. Here was Mr. Soffy with an impossible love, and at home were her guests with their impossible religion. Everything seemed in the wrong place.

As they left the vacant hall together, the moon was up in all her glory. The road before them was lit with a soft radiance.

"Let us walk awhile before I take you home," said Mr. Soffy. "The night is wonderful, and I want to talk to you."

"I think not to-night, Mr. Soffy, unless—you really *must* talk to me," Venna answered, her feelings as contradictory as her words.

"Yes, it is for your good," he replied quietly.

Venna was relieved—and with the relief, she condemned herself. The idea of her having a shade of a thought that he would speak of love.

They walked on in silence for a few moments. The night was wonderfully alluring.

"A perfect night for lovers!" thought Mr. Soffy, glancing at Venna, who was drinking in the beauty of the scene with a rapt expression. "How beautiful she is!"

"If human hearts were only as peaceful as nature!" remarked Venna quietly.

"You forget, Mrs. Hadly. To-night is wonderfully serene, to-morrow may bring a storm that will transform nature into wildness."

"That is very true," returned Venna. "After all, there is a great analogy between the spiritual and the material. I can see how the Christian Scientists can stretch the point and believe one is but the expression of the other. I wish I could accept all their doctrines. You don't know, Mr. Soffy, how I long for real concrete thinking on religious questions. If I only possessed a strong, sure belief!"

"Oh, I think you believe enough—more than I do even. I think there is greater pleasure in freedom of thought. Let your mind wander at will—you'll get more out of life. Strive to be broad, not narrow."

"Yes, I know that is the idea in the religious thought of to-day. But it doesn't somehow satisfy me. Truth is like a river, having a source and a destination. If the river broadens too much, it overflows the banks and ruins the very limitations that give it beauty."

"You ought to be a Catholic," returned Mr. Soffy, smiling.

"No, then the river would be so choked with rocks and weeds, that its course would be turbulent and without freedom."

"What would you be then?" asked Mr. Soffy, laughing. "Please don't start another sect in the Christian world. There are only hundreds now!"

"Never fear," she returned, "but I shall always long for truth, even if I never find it. What is it so important you wish to say to me?"

"It is in the way of advice and I know you will not be offended. I'm too interested in you to have you talked about. I wish to warn you."

Venna looked her surprise.

"Yes, of course, you're surprised. Women like you never see anything except through their own conceptions. It is a sure sign of your innocence. But really you must be more worldly wise."

"I don't understand you," she said, laughing. "What awful thing have I done?"

"Simply a kind Christian act, but it won't go in Ashfield. It's all over town that you are housing two Mormon preachers, as your friends, too. This labels you with everyone as 'Doubtful.' I wouldn't have a breath of scandal attached to your name, but already the village is buzzing."

"You don't mean that"—, but words failed Venna and she stopped short in angry embarrassment.

"I mean you are the subject of gossip. Gossip grows like a weed here. I hate to wound you, Mrs. Hadly, but it's for your own good. Didn't you notice your girls hurrying off to-night? They take it as a big joke, and without meaning it, they'll make things worse for you. I overheard them planning to be the first to tell Miss Harriet and Miss Mary how fine the Mormon preachers were and how they were all going to call to-morrow. They take a delight in shocking the old ladies, who won't stand shocking. I know them. I live with them, you know."

"So this is the real character of the simple life I admired so much!" exclaimed Venna, in a tone more sad than angry. "How disappointing human nature is!"

"Not if you expect little—then you find a great deal of good in people. You should never start life with too high a standard for people to measure up to. The idealist is always disappointed. The 'simple life' attracted you. You didn't realize any 'hidden depths' here, did you? Wherever man is, city or country, there will you find his same old weaknesses side by side with his nobler aspirations. You must learn to guard your actions more carefully than your thoughts."

"What would you advise me to do?" she asked seriously. She felt a happiness in his protecting interest in her welfare.

"Get rid of those fanatic Mormons first thing to-morrow, and laugh off the rumor that they are your friends."

"Oh, but I have asked them to stay for a week and thoroughly explain their beliefs to me. They claim they can give me proof of their doctrines from the Bible. They're real tired, too. Their visit would do us mutual good."

"You don't mean you have planned such a thing with strangers—and men that are talked about as they are!" replied Mr. Soffy with real concern. "Why, you haven't the least idea what people will say of you."

"Is the world so evil-minded?" returned Venna. "Then of what value is the world's opinion? What would you think of me, Mr. Soffy?"

Mr. Soffy smiled with pleasure. "Does my opinion count more than the world's? I would say, you're the truest-hearted little woman in town!"

"I only care for the opinion of good people—like you," she added softly.

"Thank you," he returned seriously.

There was a moment's silence in which both were very thoughtful.

At last Venna said quietly, "Thank you for your advice, Mr. Soffy. It was well meant. But I wish to hear what these good young men have to say. I shall keep them with me one week, regardless of Ashfield. Come, we will not walk more to-night. See, the clouds are beginning to come already. As you say, to-morrow may bring a storm."

They walked back to the house in silence again. Mr. Soffy was anxious to speak of his love to her. It was an ideal night, an ideal time. But something held him back. He was not sure of her love yet. She was too friendly, too frank. He might spoil it all. It was hard to wait, but he must be sure. So he reached the little white gate without the avowal he had intended.

Frankly she held out her hand to him.

"Good-night, Mr. Soffy. Call and see my friends, won't you?" she said, smiling.

"I certainly will. I'd like to hear them myself. I may step in to-morrow."

"Any excuse was worth while, to see her," he thought.

And so they parted for the night, she with increased admiration for his goodness, and he with increased passion for her beauty and personality.

CHAPTER IX.

To be popular in the religious world today, one must smile upon any creed; believe nothing absolutely, and regard "Truth" as too delicate a thing to be handled.

The next day did bring a storm. It was just after lunch, and Venna was sitting in the living-room with the two preachers, earnestly discussing points of doctrine. Baby Anna sat in her high chair, happily surveying the party, as each one of whom gave her occasional amusement.

"Just think of a dear babe like that being considered a sinner," remarked Brother Johnson with a tender smile at Anna.

Anna smiled her approval at this remark and held out her chubby hand to be kissed.

"You're right," returned Venna, kissing the tiny fingers. "She's a little angel— all babes are. It's a repulsive thought to connect them with the sins of this world."

"Then it won't be hard for you to accept our doctrine of pre-existence," said Brother Hallock. "It is a beautiful revelation, given to us, I think, to inspire us to live up to our origin. We know that we are the spirit children of our heavenly Father and that we come to this world fresh from His loving care. Babies need no baptism. The early Church never thought of such a thing. Infant baptism came along with other man-made doctrines, when the Church began to apostatize from the truth."

"You will not have to persuade me of that doctrine. It is so natural and you have given me enough verses in the Bible to prove it. Let us take up the future existence."

At this moment, the bell rang and Stella opened the door to Mr. Soffy. He entered with a genial smile to all. Venna was delighted. How fair-minded he was not to share everyone's prejudice concerning the Mormons!

"We're so glad you have come, Mr. Soffy," she exclaimed happily, after the usual introductions. "We are just discussing doctrines."

"Don't let me disturb you; I shall enjoy listening."

Both young men looked pleased.

"Now," said Venna, "we were talking of the *future* existence. You say there is more than one heaven? Was that a revelation, too?"

"Yes, but the Bible substantiates this revelation as it does the others." Brother Hallock gave a number of scriptural texts, and then turned to Mr. Soffy for his opinion.

"Your arguments are good," Mr. Soffy answered, "but I couldn't conceive of more than one heaven. I think I would have to see them to believe."

"Couldn't you take the word of St. Paul who did see? You know the Bible tells us that Paul not only saw *Paradise*, but was carried to the *third* heaven. Have you ever thought of that statement of Paul's?"

"Yes, I have," returned Mr. Soffy seriously "But when it comes to those mystical experiences couldn't those early Christians have had delusions?"

"You don't believe, then, that the Bible is the inspired Word of God?"

"Not entirely—no, that is rather an old-fashioned belief."

"Then," said Brother Hallock, seriously, "it is no use for us to discuss. If one believes in the inspiration of the Bible, he can easily believe in revelation. Those two beliefs coupled together lay the foundation for our proofs. There is only one other way that you could accept our truths. That is by the testimony of the Holy Ghost."

"That is rather vague testimony," returned Mr. Soffy, smiling. "I must confess, much as I like to hear your beliefs, there is small chance of my accepting any of them. I belong to the new class of thinkers who pin their understanding to very little."

Venna was watching the two and feeling the contrast of character. Brother Hallock's face shone with the power of strong convictions. Mr. Soffy smiled with the tolerance of a wandering faith.

"However," added Mr. Soffy pleasantly, "Mrs. Hadly is a firm believer in the inspiration of the Bible from cover to cover, so she will be more apt to grasp your ideas."

"Yes, indeed," Venna said with a quiet reverence; "the Bible is God's Word to me. I have a testimony within me of that truth. I can't entirely explain it, but I know that testimony is of God, too."

"Spiritual things are spiritually discerned," returned Brother Hallock. "Thank God, you have that testimony to build upon."

Again the bell rang and Stella opened the door to the girls. They were all together, a pretty, laughing bunch. On seeing Mr. Soffy, they stopped at the door, suddenly quiet.

"You're not afraid of him?" Bessie disdainfully whispered.

"Come in, girls," called Mr. Soffy, pleasantly. So the girls came in, feeling somewhat abashed, now that they were really there.

Venna welcomed them, and introduced them one by one.

"We hope we are not intruding," said Bessie demurely.

"Oh, no," returned Venna, "I want you to meet my friends. We were discussing doctrines of their Church. You may learn something."

"Oh, how interesting!" returned Bessie, the other girls remaining bashfully silent.

"The storm has made it very dark. Let us pull down the shades and light up," said Venna.

They were soon all cozily seated, oblivious to the storm without.

"Mrs. Hadly," said Brother Hallock, earnestly, "we are all Christians here. Would you not like us to have a little cottage prayer-meeting? I think it would help us all to discern truth."

"Yes, indeed," answered Venna.

And so the girls came for fun and found only two very earnest young men whose very presence seemed to bring one nearer to God. Mr. Soffy opened the meeting with prayer, after which Brother Hallock and Brother Johnson spoke alternately upon the faith of the Mormons. Venna listened hungrily. Every word they uttered fell with a decision which spoke of absolute conviction. There were no "may-bes" or waverings here. Inspired by their religion, their words flowed easily and surely.

The girls listened with wonder, not understanding everything perfectly but feeling the power of the speakers.

Mr. Soffy watched them in pleased surprise, appreciating their personalities, but scarcely considering their beliefs.

"The Spirit of God is with them," Venna said within her heart. She was the only one who was searching the truth of their words. But with this eagerness for truth, came the powerful testimony to her soul, that here at last she was to find it.

God works in mysterious ways. The searcher for truth may follow Reason until he is lost in a maze of doctrines. Hopeless he stands, but if the Faith of God is in his heart the everlasting promise is fulfilled at last, and the testimony of the Holy Ghost carries the soul beyond all of Reason's confusion. Then the soul looks back upon the intricate trodden paths, and from its heights it views Reason in a true perspective, and can choose the way to be retrodden in safety.

Oh, if the world could only realize the value of that spiritual uplift that illumines Reason, and without which Reason is a snare.

When the closing prayer had been said by Brother Johnson, there was a hushed silence for a few moments. All felt in some measure the power of the moment.

Mr. Soffy was the first to speak. He held out his hand to Brother Hallock.

"Faith like yours is worth having," he said earnestly. "I hope you can always keep it. I could never possess it, but it commands admiration."

Both the young men flushed with pleasure as they took his hand.

"This from a minister of the orthodox church is indeed a happy surprise," returned Brother Hallock.

"We are not all narrow," returned Mr. Soffy, even more pleasantly as he noticed Venna's evident approval.

Meantime, out in the storm, returning from some parish calls, were Miss Mary and Miss Harriet in their buggy. As they neared Mrs. Hadly's home, both peered out curiously.

"All the shades are drawn. I wonder what's going on inside," remarked Mary.

"I've a good mind to drop in accidentally and see for myself," returned Miss Harriet briskly. "You just hold the reins, Mary."

For an old lady, she was unusually spry. She jumped from her carriage and ascended the steps with her head held high. Sharply she rang the bell. Stella opened rather cautiously. She didn't like the tone of the bell.

"Oh, it's you, Miss Haskell, is it? Come right in," said Stella.

"Who did you think it was?" queried Miss Harriet suspiciously.

"I don't know," returned Stella nervously. "They're all in the living room. Go right in, Miss Haskell."

"All! Who's all?" thought Miss Harriet.

But she lost no time in conjecture. She reached the door of the sitting-room, and there she stood, dum-founded. "She could hardly believe her senses," she told Miss Mary afterwards.

Mr. Soffy was holding the hands of both Mormons, Mrs. Hadly and the girls were beaming upon them, while *her* boy was saying,

"We are not all narrow."

"Evidently!" came sharply from the thin lips.

The little group turned. The thin face of Miss Harriet looked down upon them with a spirit in sharp contrast to what they had been enjoying. Anger, disgust, intolerance were expressed in her cutting glance.

Mr. Soffy flushed like a truant school-boy. The girls looked pleased, the young strangers serious.

Venna controlled herself with an effort.

"Won't you come in. Miss Haskell? I want to introduce you to my *friends*."

With this the girls smiled outright.

Miss Harriet eyed them with increased anger.

"I don't care to meet your *friends*" she returned, icily. "Mr. Soffy, will you kindly escort me home?"

Mr. Soffy turned to Venna. "Will you kindly excuse me, Mrs. Hadly?"

"Certainly," returned Venna, thinking how wonderfully kind he was to Miss Harriet when she was so rude.

Miss Harriet turned without another word, and majestically sailed out of the house, followed by Mr. Soffy.

Brother Hallock followed the minister with a keen glance.

As the door outside closed, Venna turned to the girls who were exchanging glances.

"I guess, dears, you had better go now. It is getting late, and your mothers might be looking for you."

Bessie spoke up indignantly, "It's a perfect shame for that old fogie to insult you and your friends. *We* will tell our mothers all about it and she'll be treated cool by *us*, anyway."

"Don't make trouble, dear. Just act as though nothing happened. After such a lovely meeting we must bear no ill-will."

"Not on *our* account, surely," said Brother Hallock. "We are so used to such treatment, we feel only pity for our enemies."

So the girls left, promising to come again.

Outside, Bessie turned to her companions.

"I thought it would be a great lark to have just this happen, but somehow it's not much fun to have those men treated so. Aren't they wonderful? Let's defend them all over town."

"We sure will!" the girls answered.

And so youth and old age started at precisely the same moment, to arouse opposite sentiments in Ashfield, for Venna's Mormon friends.

CHAPTER X.

To a materialist, a miracle is an impossible contradiction to Nature. To the spiritually minded, it is the expression of that Higher Power which controls Nature.

Until Anna and her husband came home, Venna found herself entirely alone with her visitors. Those were two days to be remembered. It was steadily storming without, so they all stayed indoors, and talked and discussed from morning until night. Doubts in her mind that had remained unanswered for years, these two young preachers answered satisfactorily, always going to the Bible to show the authority for their claims.

Venna's interest pleased them and they never tired of her constant queries.

"You have great patience," said Venna, smiling.

"It takes no patience to answer questions," returned Brother Hallock. "The patience is required when no one is interested enough to ask them."

The third day brought Mr. and Mrs. Halloway home. Venna's explanations about the Mormons quite satisfied them.

"Of course, you were right, dear," said Anna in her big-hearted way. "The very idea of their being treated so! Why, we met a number of Mormons when we were West. They are very fine people, indeed. But don't let them take your thoughts away from Christian Science. I don't know much about 'Mormonism' but I imagine it's not at all spiritual."

"On the contrary," returned Venna, very enthusiastically, "it makes one live in a wonderfully spiritual atmosphere!"

"I'm afraid you're being influenced," said Anna anxiously.

"I'm afraid I am," admitted Venna, smiling.

"Oh, dear me! We must place their belief side by side with Christian Science. I'll keep them here until you see I can prove to them they're wrong. We'll have some good arguments—respecting one another, of course!"

"No one could help respecting you!" exclaimed Venna, delighted with the thought of delving deeper into truth.

But the discussions were unfortunately postponed.

The day after Anna's arrival, baby Anna became very ill. Mr. Halloway and Venna both wanted to send for the doctor, but Anna wouldn't hear of it.

"Do you think God will forgive me if I refuse to trust my precious lamb to His care?" she asked, trying to be calm and true to her Christian Science teachings. "This is my test—my first test of faith!"

All day, and all night, Anna knelt by her babe in prayer.

The next morning, little Anna was worse.

Mr. Halloway had to go to the city, and for the first time, he was angry with his wife.

"Anna, you see to it that you have a doctor today. I insist upon it!" and so he left her.

Anna buried her head in the bed-clothes and wept.

"O God!" she murmured, "tell me—should I obey?"

It was an agonizing morning for Anna. She did not admit even Venna to the room, but prayed unceasingly. Her momentary doubt had left her as soon as her husband's presence was gone.

Downstairs, Brother Johnson and Brother Hallock tried to console Venna.

"Oh, but if baby Anna dies without a doctor, it is too awful to think of," exclaimed Venna. "What ought I to do? *Compel* her to have one?"

"It is *her* child," said Brother Hallock seriously.

"Yes, but she will never forgive herself afterwards."

"I can't advise you, Mrs. Hadly. It is very sad, indeed. When Mr. Halloway comes home, I think he will take the matter in his own hands."

There was a sound of crying outside, and Venna recognized Bud's tearful tones and Bessie's soothing voice.

Venna stepped to the door to admit her young friends.

"Bud, dear, what is the matter?" she exclaimed as Bud entered in sobs, with Bessie's protecting arms about him.

"My—my—cat—Missus Hadly—my cat—she died of salvation—way out in the woods—with me—here—an' never knowin'!"

"What does he mean?" asked Venna of Bessie, who was trying to look sympathetic.

"Why, Bud's pussie got lost in the woods, and never came back for weeks. Now he's found her dead, so he thinks it was starvation killed her."

"Yes, an' I'll never—pump—the organ in Mr. Soffy's church again, 'cause I don't like religion any more. I prayed that Flip would come home, an' a lot o' good prayin' does!"

Bud was inconsolable. Venna told him he must not talk that way. God knew why Flip had to be taken from him.

"That's jes' it! An' that's why I won't pump that organ any more!"

Venna turned to Bessie.

"I can't visit with you now, dear. Did you know baby was very sick?"

"Baby is sick, is she?" spoke up Bud. "How'd you feel if *she* died?"

Venna trembled at the suggestion.

"We must all pray for her to get well. Bud."

"A lot o' good prayin' ull do!" declared Bud defiantly. "Did it help Flip? You better git the doctor hustlin' or she'll be a goner, too. Seems ter me there's lots a dyin' goin' on."

"There, there! Bud! Run along and ask Stella for some real sugar cookies. They'll change your thoughts."

"Never! Think I'm thet mean ter eat sugar cookies the day Flip died o' salvation? Ter-night—yer may see me helpin' round. Good-bye!"

Her visitors gone, Venna excused herself from the young missionaries and went upstairs. Perhaps she could persuade Anna.

Gently she knocked at the door, but there was no response.

She quietly opened it. There upon the floor lay Anna, white and motionless. Trembling, Venna knelt by her side.

"Anna, dear Anna!" she exclaimed, shaking her gently.

But there was no response.

Venna hurried downstairs and phoned for the doctor to come at once.

"May I go up and try to revive her?" asked Brother Hallock.

Together they went up to Anna's room. Brother Hallock looked from the prostrate mother to the moaning babe.

"My! This is sad!" he exclaimed. "But don't worry. Let us bathe her head. She has fainted with exhaustion, that is all."

Anna soon opened her eyes, and looked around with a dazed, helpless expression.

"Baby! baby! Where is she, Venna? Have they taken her away?"

"No, dear, she is right here on the bed. We'll help you to the couch and you must lie perfectly still. I'll take care of baby. The doctor is coming, Anna."

"As you say," returned Anna, too weak to resist, and again she swooned as she was being helped to the couch.

Venna felt great relief when the bell rang and the old village doctor appeared. Entering the room brusquely, he made a general survey. First he went to Anna.

"Revive her again quickly, and give her plenty of hot milk. Worn out, that's all."

Then he went to baby Anna. After a careful examination, he turned to Venna and slowly shook his head.

"I need a consultation here. This is a serious case—very serious."

Venna paled.

"O Dr. Jensen! consult with the best doctor you know. Is there time to get one from New York?"

"No!" declared Dr. Jensen, "she must be attended to quickly, or you'll lose her to-night. It *may* be paralysis."

Venna's heart beat wildly.

"Oh, no! no! Don't say it is that awful disease!"

She had been reading the papers, telling of the little ones dying daily in New York.

"We'll *hope* not. I'll not lose a moment. I'll go myself after Dr. Becker." And he hurried off.

Brother Hallock looked at the babe in serious thought. This was a time when the Lord could show these good women the power given to His servants.

Venna was speaking soothing words to Anna, who was again regaining consciousness.

"O Venna, if baby should die, I would never forgive myself," she murmured brokenly.

Venna's ready tears came.

"My dear Anna, be brave. God can save her even now. Have faith."

"What has my faith done for me?" she asked bitterly.

Brother Hallock quietly withdrew and joined his companion.

It seemed a long time before Dr. Jensen returned. In reality it was only half an hour.

The two doctors consulted long and earnestly.

In the adjoining room Venna and Anna awaited their decision fearfully.

Finally they were called and looked into the serious faces of the two doctors with anxious questioning.

Dr. Jensen cleared his throat and then spoke huskily.

"My dear ladies, we regret to tell you, there is no hope. The child cannot live many hours. It is paralysis."

Dr. Jensen caught Anna as again she swooned.

"Don't think of the child," he said brusquely, turning to Venna. "We must attend to the mother, she's in bad shape."

Dr. Jensen then gave directions to Venna, who immediately went downstairs to get the required restoratives.

Brother Hallock met her in the hall. Quickly she told him the sad news.

"Have the doctors given her up entirely?"

"Yes," returned Venna, striving to keep back her tears.

"Then may we administer to the child?"

"For what?" asked Venna puzzled.

"For recovery," returned the young missionary. "You have sought man's aid. Will you refuse God's?"

"But Anna tried faith?" returned Venna.

"Sometimes faith is so strong that it works even in error. But it is not God's way. God's commands are sure. If you do not believe we have His divine authority to heal, will you let us have permission to try?"

Venna looked into Brother Hallock's earnest gray eyes and felt the power of his convictions.

"Yes," she answered simply.

The doctors gone, Venna sat by Anna's bed, soothing the tired head in its restless forced sleep, the result of Dr. Jensen's quieting medicine.

In the next room she heard the missionaries, moving quietly as they administered to baby Anna.

A great unaccountable peace suddenly came over her, and she felt the presence of Divinity surrounding her.

"Surely there are guardian angels, as Brother Hallock teaches," she thought with a sudden great joy.

She looked up. Brother Hallock stood in the doorway. He motioned her to come. She arose and followed him to the bed of baby Anna.

Could it be possible? Was she dreaming? There lay the wee babe, looking up at her with its sweet, winsome baby smile.

"You have saved her," exclaimed Venna in joyous gratitude.

"We have done nothing. God has saved her. We are but the humble instruments in His hands!"

CHAPTER XI.

"I wonder if St. Peter at the Gate of Heaven will distinguish between the 'Pious' and the 'Godly'?"—Irony of Boss Holden.

Bud lost no time in circulating the news that baby Anna was sick, and would doubtless die like Flip. Due to the character of the "simple life," most of the women forgot their prejudices and only thought that some neighbor was in trouble, so those that did not immediately run up to the house, at any rate phoned to see what they could do.

Brother Hallock and Stella were kept busy answering the phone or door bell, and delivering messages to Venna.

"How kind hearted they are after all!" exclaimed Venna, gratefully.

When Dr. Jensen came back to see Venna about quarantining the house, he was amazed to find her all smiles.

"O Dr. Jensen," she said joyously, admitting him, "baby is fine and Mrs. Halloway is almost in hysterics with joy."

"I don't understand you," said Dr. Jensen, looking dazed.

"Come and see!" exclaimed Venna.

He followed her upstairs to the room he had left such a short time ago.

Here in the little bed lay baby Anna, laughing at her toes. Beside her, sat Anna, with tears of joy streaming down her face.

"I'll be—!" But he checked his exclamation as he looked at Venna, dumfounded.

"You may well be surprised. Doctor. But with God nothing is impossible."

"I—I must have made a mistake—but yet—we were both so sure; strange! It's beyond me!"

Then Venna told him about the young preachers' gift of healing.

"Pooh! Nonsense!" exclaimed Dr. Jensen. "Don't let yourself believe such nonsense! Well, I must hurry off to the Board of Health and confess that we made our first mistake. It couldn't have been paralysis!"

So Dr. Jensen reported his error to the authorities, but Anna and Venna thanked God for the miracle.

When Mr. Halloway returned he was told the wonderful story. But, contrary to their expectations, he was not at all sceptical.

"I saw her this morning and I see her tonight," he said, very much impressed. "*That* is what I call *proof!*"

Anna and Venna asked the young preachers to prolong their stay.

"Both of us—and Mr. Halloway also, want to understand your beliefs thoroughly."

So the young missionaries consented to stay until they had given their message to its fullest extent.

When Bud spread the story of baby Anna's miraculous recovery, sentiment swayed like a pendulum, and the prejudice, temporarily overcome by sympathy, now asserted itself with greater force. Mr. Allworth was seen talking to groups of his parishioners and always gravely shaking his head.

"It is the work of Satan," he declared more than once.

He even felt it his duty to call upon Miss Haskell and consult with her upon this awful menace that had entered Ashfield!

"Is there no legal way of putting these young men out of town?" asked Mr. Allworth.

"Not unless you can persuade Mayor Holden they are doing mischief. It's hard to convince a man like him who is so worldly and not in touch with the Lord."

"Yes," spoke up Miss Mary piously, "but we might pray before attempting to convince him."

"You are right," said Miss Harriet with decision, "I'll go to him myself. Though he did insult me in his store, I'll show him I'm not afraid of him!"

So the "trio" prayed, after which Miss Harriet set out upon her dutiful errand. It was in the afternoon, so she would have a chance to see him alone. Sure enough, as she entered the store, there sat the postmaster, proprietor and Mayor, making out his monthly post-office report for Washington. Not a soul was in the store.

Boss Holden looked up with an inward groan. His monthly report was anything but pleasant, and here was Miss Harriet! He could tell by her expression that she had official business to transact!

"What can I do for you?" he asked, with rough kindness.

"I've come, Mayor Holden, to enter a protest against those young Mormon preachers remaining in town!"

"What have they done?" asked Holden, laying down his pen, and settling back in his chair comfortably.

His simple question and keen glance disconcerted Miss Haskell for a moment. Then she felt the fighting spirit rise within her.

"What *haven't* they done. Mayor Holden? They've gained such an influence over the young girls, I believe they'd all leave for Utah tomorrow, if asked, and they're spreading around town that they saved baby Anna from certain death. *If* they did, it was, because Satan helped them to it. Are all our labors in the churches to come to naught, while you sit calmly by and say nothing, 'till it's too late?"

Boss Holden smiled unpleasantly.

"To put the complaint in a nutshell. Miss Harriet, they've really done nothing yet, except get themselves liked and saved a baby! Can't oust them on that!"

"You refuse, then, to put them out?" asked Miss Harriet, stiffening with righteous scorn. "I can plainly see, Mayor Holden, how you never could enter a church! If you encourage evil influence here, you have no right to be Mayor of Ashfield!"

"Perhaps you'd like the job?" asked Mayor Holden, with rising anger.

"When women get the vote, they may have such opportunity," returned Miss Harriet, sharply. "I ask you again, do you refuse?"

"Damm't, I do! And I hope those decent fellows will stay here long enough to hand out their influence. To hell with all this gossip!"

Miss Haskell shuddered.

"Such language in the presence of a lady! I might have expected it. Well, Mayor Holden, if *you* won't do your duty, *I* shall!"

And with great dignity she left the store.

Holden mopped his brow with his handkerchief.

"What fool trick will she be up to now?" he muttered. "Join that church bunch? Guess not, Holden! You have too much respect for yourself," he chuckled.

Miss Harriet, Miss Mary and Mr. Allworth united forces in their great cause of duty toward Ashfield. They sent out notices to their neighbors, writing both mothers and fathers to attend meetings, in which the trio took turns in disclosing the "awful evils" in the "Mormon Menace." No children or young girls were admitted. The parents were horrified at the disclosures.

At these meetings, Mr. Allworth exerted his influence in true Methodist style. With tears and pleadings, he begged the people to "Beware!" The response was quick and decisive. They forbade their girls to go near Mrs. Hadly. The girls sullenly obeyed, but openly defended "The Mormons." This intensified the impression of the diabolical influence they possessed.

Meanwhile, all unconscious of the village murmurings, Venna, Anna and her husband were enjoying their visitors to the utmost. Anna's deep gratitude for the recovery of her babe helped the young missionaries in their convincing arguments.

Both Venna and Anna demanded Biblical proof for all doctrines. But Mr. Halloway accepted Mormonism after a few short talks.

"You go on reasoning, Anna," he said kindly, "but I've got enough proof right here in these two young men themselves. If ever God was with men. He's with these two. Haven't I seen enough of the world to know they have something different to other men? I've led the practical life and have learned to know men directly I meet them. They couldn't fool me. These men are not doing Satan's work. How do I know it? Because I *know men*. Now, if they're not of Satan, they have to be of God—or how did they save our babe? That's all the reasoning I want. I'm ready to have them *teach me* religion now. Thank God, there's some real religion in the world—something *substantial* to work on!"

Venna wondered at the girls' absence, but was too busy to give it much thought.

Toward the end of the week Bud came in the back door with a mysterious caution.

"Say, Stella, don't yer squeal I've been here. I want ter see Missus Hadly alone!"

"Come here. Bud," called Venna from the sitting room, as she heard his voice.

Bud entered cautiously, his eyes round with wonder.

"An' yer sitting here so calm like!" he exclaimed in open admiration.

"And why not, Bud dear?" she asked, laughing.

"Yer too good for Ashfield, Missus Hadly!" said Bud, gingerly touching one of her curls. "The divil's got holt o' this place!"

"What do you mean, Bud?"

"I mean I come ter warn yer an' yer friends. There's goin' ter be a des-tin-ation ter-night."

"Destination? You've got your big word wrong again. Bud. Use a smaller one."

"I tho't a big game ought ter hev a big word. Well, there's goin' ter be a show down o' feeling."

"Oh, you mean demonstration. I see—well, a demonstration of what feeling. Bud?"

"Feeling agin the Mormon fellers! Outside yer house ter night! I overheard Mister Allworth talking wi' Miss Harriet. I'll never like a minister again! Nasty, mean, isn't it?"

Venna looked serious. "Tell me *everything* you heard, Bud."

"Heard only words now an' then. I almost fell off the roof a' listenin'. Mother'll paddle me if she finds me here. Must be goin'. This house is got an awful name—all for nuthin', jes 'cause angels like you ain't the style no more."

Venna put her arms around Bud and hugged him close.

"You blessed lambie—if all the world were as fair as you!" she exclaimed, kissing both his round cheeks, much to Bud's pleasure.

"Run along now, dear. Don't get in trouble about us. You're good to warn us—we'll be prepared? Sugar cookies in the kitchen, you know!"

When Bud left her, Venna stood for a moment in troubled thought. "Is it possible that *Christians* can do these things to those who love the same God?" she asked, for the first time coming in conflict with the religious intolerance of the day. She had blissfully imagined that religious intolerance was a thing of the past. But Venna was only upon the threshold of religious experience.

CHAPTER XII.

When we undertake to defend Christendom we often assist the devil.

It was almost dark when the Halloways, Venna and the missionaries had finished their evening meal. Venna decided to say nothing about Bud's information, as doubtless the warning grew out of his own imagination after hearing some unfavorable comments upon the "Mormons." No doubt the village was hating them. Brother Hallock said most of the Eastern people believed the lies circulated about the Church.

Venna felt a little uneasy as they all went into the sitting room. Suppose Bud had spoken the truth?

"Oh, it couldn't be," she decided.

She pulled down the shades and turned on the lights. She felt a strange comfort tonight in shutting out the outside world. Soon she was entertaining them with her violin. Never did she play better. Her music expressed her mixed feelings—now sad, now questioning, now joyously triumphant. Brother Hallock watched her with a wrapt expression, entirely lost to his surroundings.

At last her notes died away in a gentle trembling pianissimo. No one spoke as she laid down her violin. For a few moments each one enjoyed the spell of her genius.

Venna seated herself by the window and, drawing the shade aside, looked out. Suddenly she started. Coming down the hill, she saw a large group of about forty villagers, led by Mr. Allworth and Miss Harriet. What did it mean? She thought of Bud. She watched them as they approached. They were all talking excitedly.

"What interests you, Venna?" asked Anna.

"Quite a crowd are coming this way," she said, anxiously, as she turned to her friends. "I fear from what Bud said today, they are antagonistic to Brother Johnson and Brother Hallock."

"They are, are they?" spoke up Mr. Halloway brusquely, as he arose, went to the window and looked out. "Just let them utter any sentiments around here, and there will be trouble."

"Oh, dear, please don't pay any attention to them," pleaded Anna. "We'll lock the doors and not answer the bell at all. We are not interested in what *they* think."

The young missionaries looked serious.

"I'm sorry we've brought trouble to you good people," said Brother Hallock.

"You've brought us everything good; it's these people who bring us the bad," returned Halloway, as he went out to secure the locks.

The crowd had neared the house and as Halloway re-entered the sitting-room, the bell rang loudly.

"Let them ring," said Halloway in disgust. "Mayor Holden shall hear of this. He's not the kind to allow it."

"I'll go myself to the Mayor if they annoy you," said Brother Hallock.

"Oh, no! You must stay here," said Venna anxiously.

He smiled at her fears.

Once again the bell rang.

Receiving no answer, one young Methodist boy of sixteen shouted—

"Come out here, you Mormons! We want to give you your walking papers. If you don't go soon, we'll make it hot for you!"

No one made any attempt to stop the lad. He evidently expressed the opinion of the crowd.

"I'm not going to have you annoyed this way. I shall see the Mayor myself," said Brother Hallock, jumping up and going to the door.

Venna stepped in front of him and held the door fast, while the others were excitedly talking in the sitting-room, and did not notice.

"Do not open it," she said; "I fear for you."

He looked down into her anxious face with a calm smile.

"This—is nothing for us. We are used to almost any abuse. I shall never forget your kindness, though," he added earnestly.

And gently he took her hand from the door, and turning the lock, he opened it.

Standing face to face with the villagers who had crowded through the gate, he looked from side to side without a word. The dignity and fearlessness of Brother Hallock subdued them, for as he made to go down the steps, they moved apart to let him pass.

Silently he made his way through their midst, and Venna watched him walking leisurely toward Mayor Holden's, the crowd staring after him in wondering surprise.

Quickly she closed the door again.

"Well," said Miss Harriet sharply, "we all acted as though we were afraid. What's the matter with us all anyway?"

"It's the devil's power," said Mr. Allworth, shaking his head slowly. "I felt as though he cast a spell around us."

"And I, too," said Miss Mary, meekly.

"It will take more than our good intentions to get rid of that man!" declared Miss Harriet. "We'd better go home."

And so the crowd slowly turned tail. From under the stoop, a little figure bobbed up, and gazed after the retreating forms.

"Golly! That's no game fight!" said Bud, disappointed. "Tho't we'd had somethin' 'citing and could ha' used my water pistol. Gee! All he had ter do was ter look at 'em!"

The next day an official poster was put up on the post outside of Holden's store.

"Anyone attempting to annoy their neighbor, will be dealt with according to law.

"Signed

"Mayor Holden."

And at mail time Bud stationed himself beside the post, with hands thrust into pockets filled with gum-drops. As each citizen approached, he nodded his head sideways.

"See that sign? Some law here alrighty! Pity the feller thet breaks it!"

—

The afternoon after this unpleasant experience, Mr. Soffy called.

"I want to assure you, Mrs. Hadly, Miss Haskell told me nothing of her intentions—I presume because she knows I would have prevented her. I guess they all feel pretty small now, however."

"I was sure you had no knowledge of it," returned Venna, seriously. "But I do think your influence in this matter is needed. Won't you defend these two good men at your morning service next Sunday?"

"I—I—hardly think I could do *that*," returned Mr. Soffy, coloring to his temples. "You see, Mrs. Hadly, *I* know they are fine men, but to declare the fact in the little church would cause considerable antagonism and really do no good."

"The declaration of truth *always* does good *finally*."

"Well, yes, figuratively speaking, but we ministers have to be practical, too, you know."

"Mr. Soffy, what avails the Church if it countenances error? I thought *you* were above that 'worldly wisdom' reasoning!" she said, looking up into his face with great disappointment.

How beautiful she was as she stood pleading the cause of the Mormons! His whole soul thrilled with the perfection of her! If he should sacrifice a little materially, what was that to gaining her love?

"And if I should grant you this request, what would *you* do for me?" he asked, smiling down at her.

"Oh, anything you could ask of me!" she declared in extravagant delight.

Before Venna realized what had happened, his arm had encircled her waist and his kiss was upon her cheek.

Venna drew back quickly and faced him in astonished anger.

"How dare you!" she said, trembling like a frightened child.

"I *dare* because I love you, Venna. God knows how much. It's the *best* that's in me that loves you, not the worst. It is not my fault that I love you, or that you love me, as I believe you do. You resent my love from duty, don't you? You think I'll think less of you if you love me? No, dear, love is love's excuse. The world wouldn't understand, but the world needn't know. You and I can love ideally without the aid of the law, can't we?"

Venna listened to this man, and watched his fine eloquent eyes convey his devotion to her while speaking. There was no doubting his sincerity.

What a paradox! A Christian minister asking love of a married woman without a twinge of conscience! Surely the world was whirling around and morality was simply a question mark!

Steadily she looked at him in silence, trying to fathom his nature and understand.

"You are angry with me?" he asked gently.

"No, Mr. Soffy, I don't think I am. But I *pity* you; oh! how I pity you!" she said sadly.

"You don't *love* me, then?" he asked in a tone of agitation and fear.

"No, Mr. Soffy, I don't even *respect* you."

"Why?" he asked, his pride clearly hurt.

"I hardly think *you* could understand," returned Venna sadly. "There is a great barrier between us, a barrier of spiritual understanding. I realize your sin. You do not."

"Wherein have I sinned?" he asked. "Is it a sin to devote one's life to his ideal, and love her above all else?"

"Yes," returned Venna, "when we love her more than our duty."

"And what *is* duty?" he asked, cynically.

"Ask your God, Mr. Soffy. He will answer you so that you may understand. Good-bye," she added, holding out her hand.

He took it and pressed it hard.

"When can I see you again?" he asked eagerly.

"Never, Mr. Soffy."

"You don't mean *that*?" he asked, growing suddenly pale.

"Yes," she answered simply, looking at him with a great pity in her lovely eyes.

Without a word, he slowly dropped her hand and left her.

She looked from the window and watched him walk down the steps, his head bowed in thought.

When he reached the gate, he met Brother Hallock. The two shook hands and exchanged a few words.

"What a contrast!" thought Venna, watching the two men. "The one sacrificing all for duty—the other sacrificing duty for self!"

Brother Hallock came directly into the room to Venna.

"Mrs. Hadly, Brother Johnson and myself have decided to resume our journey tomorrow."

"Oh, we will all be so disappointed if you go so soon," returned Venna, suddenly feeling that she needed this man's presence.

"We couldn't think of staying after the affair last night. It wouldn't be fair to you. Besides, our duty calls us away now. You know we missionaries are not out to enjoy ourselves," he added, smiling.

"There are so many things I want to ask you yet," she said, hoping she might detain him a few days longer.

"And we will be so glad to answer them. Uncle Sam's post-office will handle our correspondence, I hope. We will never forget you all, and when you return to New York, we will call, and I will introduce you to our Mission President's family and other saints. I know you will enjoy our meetings."

"I *know* I shall," returned Venna, happy in the thought. "I appreciate your religion more and more by contrasting it with others," she added.

"It will bear the light," replied Brother Hallock seriously. He looked at her intently a moment and then added, "No good thing needs to be hidden in the dark. Only *evil* fears the light."

Venna dropped her eyes. Could it be possible he divined Mr. Soffy's love for her?

She felt his persistent gaze. She raised her eyes and fearlessly met his.

"I agree with you, Brother Hallock. I hope God will always give me power to make my life an open book!"

He gave a quick sigh of relief.

"Thank God for that sentiment!" he returned earnestly.

CHAPTER XIII.

The happiness derived from doing our duty is the greatest joy the world affords.

"How I miss Brother Hallock and Brother Johnson!" exclaimed Anna, as she and Venna settled down to a quiet afternoon with their sewing and books.

"Yes, we will all miss their influence—even babe," returned Venna, looking at little Anna playing on her pillow.

Baby smiled her assent.

Anna leaned over and kissed her.

"My precious little angel!" she said, hugging her wee one tight. "You know, Venna, I always called her 'angel,' but now my pet name for her has a significance!"

"Yes," replied Venna, "how much more beautiful life seems, now that we have learned so many wonderful truths. You know, Anna, life has a different perspective for me now. When I think of the wonderful purpose God had in placing us here and the short period of probation that our lives afford us, I have no other thought than to do my highest duty."

"And that is?" asked Anna.

"First, living up to all my vows. I know you'll be surprised at my decision. Read this letter I received this morning from Will."

Anna took the letter and read:

"Dearest Venna:

"I'm in a strange mood tonight. I feel as though life had ended for me. I don't know why I should write to *you* since you have cast me off as worthless. But somehow I'm not myself. I'm weak stuff to write to one who despises me. But love makes a fool of a man anyway. The counterfeit of love ruins a man's youth, and then when the real thing comes along, it's just about as bad. No satisfaction in any of it! I'd be glad to finish myself tonight—but I love you too much to create a scandal. Are you so hard that you can't even write me a friendly word? I'll be true to you, whether you love me or not. You might be at least *kind*. Write me a letter—any kind of a one, won't you?

"Venna, if you ever love a man you think good enough for you, let me know and I'll slip out. You haven't the least conception of my love for you. You're so ignorant of the world. You think of those other women. They were nothing to me. I guess you're right about men not stooping to such actions, but there are two sides to every question, Venna. They tempt the young men.

They deserve all they get. I'm sorry for my past because of you. I don't pity *them*.

"It's useless to write more. You'll write the same hard, uncompromising note in return, I suppose.

"Well, throw my devotion to the dogs if you wish. You may need it, though. If so, it's yours.

"Always your devoted husband,

"Will."

As Anna handed back the letter to Venna, her eyes were filled with tears.

"There's lots of good in your husband, Venna," she said seriously.

"And I am stifling it," returned Venna quietly. "In the light of the Gospel, I see myself as I really am. I'm not living to save souls, but to save myself from unpleasant experiences. Anna, I'm going back to Will."

Anna's eyes glistened through her tears.

"You dear girl! Now you've struck the right keynote to your life. God will bless you for it."

"He has already. I have never felt so happy as since I wrote this letter. Read it."

Anna read eagerly.

"Dear Will:

"I shall come home tomorrow. We will begin all over again and make our lives a success.

"Yours faithfully,

"Venna."

Anna looked up with a smile. "Wonderful, Venna! But couldn't you write 'Yours lovingly?'"

"It wouldn't be true," replied Venna, coloring.

"You can't love him then?" asked Anna doubtfully.

"No, but I love *duty*, Anna, and I'll pray God to make me love him in time. I'll do my *best*."

"You can't do more," returned her friend. "So I am to lose you also. I don't think I'll stay here long alone. I've come to dislike Ashfield so."

"It don't seem the same, does it? We mustn't forget, however, that here we received the Truth."

So the following day Venna quietly left Ashfield. None knew of her going, and as she sat in the train, bound for New York, she was thankful she was leaving the "simple life" which only two months ago she was idealizing.

At the New York station, Will Hadly met her. She felt shocked at the change in him. He was thin and pale, with that drawn look upon his face which betokened mental worry.

Her heart smote her. Pity surged within her, and she looked up at him with real concerned emotion, which he mistook for love.

"Dearest," he whispered, "I can scarcely believe my exile is over! I received your letter this morning. The servants are so delighted you're coming. They're hustling all day to make the home fit to receive their queen!"

When they reached the Fifth Avenue home, Venna entered with a strange, trembling fear. A new life was before her—a happy life, but one of sacrifice—and sacrifice was a new experience!

As they entered the door, the fragrance of roses greeted her. Everywhere flowers! Hadly had spared no expense to have the home filled with nature's best.

"A garland of roses for my bride!" he said, gaily laughing at her surprise. "And now to the feast!" he exclaimed, leading her into the dining-room. Here the daylight had been shut out, and all the lights were ablaze.

The table was set for two, with every conceivable dainty for a joyous feast.

"Does my bride approve?" he asked tenderly.

Venna looked up at him tearfully. "You couldn't have done better." was all she said.

The dinner over, Venna and her husband went into the old library. Venna looked around and vivid memories of her life filled her eyes with tears.

"What troubles you?" Hadly asked, fearing she was regretting her step.

"This room makes me think of dear father. It was almost *his* room."

"Yes, I know," returned Hadly, relieved. "Look over your shoulder, you will see a present for my bride."

Venna turned and there upon the wall, she beheld a life-sized portrait of her father, gazing down upon them, with an almost life-like smile.

"O Will!" she exclaimed.

She could say nothing more, but moved slowly to the picture and stood gazing up at the familiar face with an expression of intense yearning. She did not even hear the bell.

Hadly heard it, however, and stepped to the hall.

"We see no one tonight," he instructed the servant. Then he quietly closed the door and stepped over to Venna's side. Putting his arm about her, he gently drew her to him.

"You like it?" he asked, pleased.

"Oh, it was so thoughtful of you!" she exclaimed gratefully. "I can feel his presence here tonight."

The door opened so quietly that neither one noticed it.

Hadly stooped and kissed Venna.

A loud laugh made them turn suddenly.

"The kiss of death!" mocked a woman's voice in scorn.

There in the doorway stood a woman heavily veiled.

She leveled a pistol at Hadly and a loud shot followed.

Her aim was true. Hadly fell heavily at Venna's feet. The woman turned and fled.

No sound escaped Venna's lips. White as death she stooped and gently lifted his head. The servants, hearing the shot, rushed in. She ordered them to summon aid. In fear and trembling they instantly obeyed.

Alone with her husband, a terrible fear possessed her. Was he dead? Was she too late with her pity?

Slowly his eyes opened and looked up into her face.

"Venna girl," he whispered, "it's all over—my dream—it's a rude awakening, but it's best—best for you—Venna, my bride!"

"No! No! Will! We will save you! Have courage!"

She stooped and tenderly kissed his forehead, then gently stroked his hair.

He smiled happily.

"The kiss of death! Yes—how sweet! Good-bye, Venna—find a man worthy of the best—little"—

The sentence was never finished. When help came, they found Venna sobbing hysterically with Hadly in her arms!—dead!

CHAPTER XIV.

"Our extremity is God's opportunity."

It was just a month since Will Hadly's death.

Pale and serious in her black mourning gown, Venna sat alone in the library answering letters. This was her first opportunity, as every minute of her time had been so far taken up with lawyers.

She had found her financial affairs in excellent condition, new and careful investments having been made by her husband. However, she was surprised that his supposed fortune was entirely gone. He died penniless, having gambled away everything he possessed.

This was a sad revelation to her, but money from him was not needed. How conscientious he had been with her own!

She took up two letters from Brother Johnson and Brother Hallock. They were filled with sympathy and good advice.

In a few weeks they would be through with their country work and be living in New York.

How she longed to see them! Religious longings had grown within her since the tragic death of her husband.

She answered both letters slowly, asking many questions and requesting answers. She was in that nervous condition which makes one feel that not one minute of life can be lost, and every problem must be immediately solved.

As she was folding up these letters, the maid announced a caller.

"I can't see any one yet," said Venna, shrinking from the outside world.

"The lady told me to give you this card, and you might make an exception."

Venna took the card. "May a friend of Brother Hallock's see you a few minutes?" was informally written.

"I will see her," said Venna.

A short, stout woman entered the room and held out a friendly hand to Venna as she came forward.

"I'm so glad to meet you, dear Mrs. Hadly," she said in a quiet, pleasant voice. "Brother Hallock wrote me that you might like to have one of our faith call upon you. I hope I'm not intruding?"

"No, indeed," returned Venna, feeling a quickening influence from this bright, motherly person.

"I'm Sister Maddon. My husband is president of the —— Company, so we have to live East now. I miss the West so much, but I'm thankful we have a conference of our people here. I want you to meet all the Latter-day Saints right soon, won't you?" she asked cordially.

Venna looked down at her black dress.

"Yes, I know," continued her new friend, sitting next to Venna and taking her thin white hand in her own large, capable one. "Don't think because I don't dwell upon it, that I fail to understand your sorrow. It's kinder to help one forget and not bring sad things to the surface. It won't do anyone any good to sit at home and grieve. Let me tell you about our people here, and then perhaps you will want to meet them soon."

For the next hour Venna completely lost herself in listening to her caller's vivid description of the Eastern Conference work, its leaders and their difficulties. When the hour had passed, she felt as though she had known this woman many years. She expressed herself to this effect.

"It is the Spirit of the Lord, dear girl, that draws us together," she explained with a bright, happy smile. "The spirit of the world never does that, does it?"

"No, indeed!" exclaimed Venna. "Somehow I never shrunk from the world as I do now."

"When you have the Gospel firmly written on your heart, you will be eager to enter the world and help it."

When her visitor left, Venna promised to spend the following Saturday with her.

"No one will be there but you and I and the children. We'll have a cosy day that will take you out of yourself," assured Sister Maddon.

——

As Sister Maddon left the house, Mrs. Hansom entered.

"My dear Venna," she said, putting her arms around her niece affectionately, "you look pale as death. I insist on your packing up some things and coming home with me for a month."

"No, no! Auntie dear, I couldn't stand it, really. So many people all the time. If it were only you, dear, but"—

"Don't you know everyone understands and sympathizes with you?"

"Of course—that's just it. They sympathize and condole, until I can't stand it. Don't think I'm ungrateful, but just leave me alone for a little while. Just you come to see me, dear, and I'll come around finely."

"Who was that lady who just went out?"

Venna hesitated. She had told her aunt nothing of her Mormon faith. She hardly felt equal to her disapproval, but she couldn't deceive. It was plainly her duty to declare herself.

"Auntie dear," she said quietly, "that lady is a friend of a Mormon missionary who visited us in the country. He is a wonderful young man, and quite converted Anna, her husband and myself."

Mrs. Hansom at first look puzzled, then suddenly frightened.

"You don't mean you entertained a Mormon?"

"Yes, two of them," returned Venna, slightly smiling.

"And—and Anna allowed it?" queried her aunt, dismayed.

"Not only allowed it, but felt sad at their going." This was too awful for words. Mrs. Hansom gazed at her niece with shame and sorrow.

"You weren't influenced by such people, were you? What do you mean by 'Converted?' Wasn't your father's faith good enough for you, Venna?"

"I've lost nothing of dear father's faith," returned Venna, looking up at his picture, as her eyes became moist. "How sad it is that Christians won't understand these good Mormon people! I have simply strengthened the weak and tottering faith I possessed by learning and accepting added great truths. Oh, if you only knew these missionaries, you would feel their power!"

"Evidently you have felt their power," returned Mrs. Hansom cooly. "I never thought I would live to see this day!"

There was no anger in the keen, searching look Venna gave her aunt. She was trying to read her soul and fathom the mystery of this un-Christian attitude toward the Mormons. There seemed only one explanation.

"Auntie, those anti-Mormon lecturers, who have poisoned the minds of so many Church people, are terribly responsible before God for their lies. When Brother Hallock returns to the city, I'll have you meet him and then you'll know the truth."

"I would not have him enter my door!" returned Mrs. Hansom.

"You wouldn't, then, consider the other side?" asked Venna.

"Not in the case of the Mormons."

Venna did not answer for a moment. Her eyes wandered again to her father's picture.

"Father would have listened," she said softly.

Her aunt colored.

"Yes, I believe dear John would listen to anyone. He was too soft-hearted for this world. Yes, and in those days I would have, too, I suppose. But Dr. Hansom has taught me that compromise kills. I am much stronger for his great influence," she added with pride.

Venna looked at her aunt with a great pity. How she had changed. She seemed to reflect her husband's character as far as her weak nature would permit.

"Auntie, if you refuse to hear the defense how can you judge?"

"It isn't always well to listen to Satan's defense—it often blurs your conceptions—those are Dr. Hansom's exact words. I've heard him give them more than once."

Venna smiled in spite of herself.

"I'm talking to auntie—not to Dr. Hansom," she said kindly.

"Dr. Hansom and I think alike on all subjects," she returned firmly. "Now, Venna, I hope you'll get over this foolishness very quickly. We could never tolerate it, you know. I must get home now, for the 'Auxiliary' meeting is at my house. You won't return with me?"

"Not to-day, auntie. Please come often, won't you?"

"I'm afraid you need it, child!" exclaimed her aunt anxiously. And with a kiss and a pat of the rebellious curls, she was gone.

Venna stood in front of "Daddy's" picture and the tears streamed down both pale cheeks.

"Dear Daddy, if you were only here! You were so fair to everyone. You would understand. Oh, how I need you!"

Suddenly a great wave of happiness swept over her being. She felt a presence in the room. She turned. There in the door-way, with arms outstretched, stood Daddy, *her* Daddy, with the same old loving smile of approval and understanding.

Motionless she stood, gazing with unspeakable joy.

What a great love shone from his eyes—a protecting love that seemed to thrill her with new confidence and hope.

"Daddy!" she exclaimed and stepped toward him.

She was about to clasp his hand, but he vanished from her touch.

Venna, dazed, stood alone. But the influence of his presence remained with her. New rapturous emotion filled her breast, new hopes, new determination were hers!

She knelt down and prayed.

"O God! I thank Thee for this wonderful vision! Help me to be worthy!"

She arose from her knees with a radiant countenance.

"Daddy is not dead!" she murmured happily. "He knows! He will help me!"

CHAPTER XV.

To be popular and also truthful is beyond the power of man.

Sister Maddon was busy bustling about the kitchen, giving directions to her maid for the lunch to be prepared for their new visitor, Mrs. Hadly.

"Now, Mary, make the table look just as cheery as you can. Put the flowers at both ends, and choose the doilies with the brightest colors."

"Me, too, mudder?" piped up the three-year-old urchin tugging at her skirts.

"Yes, sugar plum, if you're awfully good and don't ask for anything at the table."

"Me good!" exclaimed the delighted child, dropping his mother's skirts and running in to tell his older sister.

"That means I'm to wash you up," said eight-year-old Eleanor, catching the youngster and smothering him with kisses.

The kitchen door opened to admit a noisy boy of ten.

"Golly! mother! Things smell good around here. Going to be a company dinner?"

"Yes, Teddy, and if you don't look just as clean as wax, you can't enter the domains!" returned his mother, smiling.

"Me for a wash-up!" exclaimed Teddy, throwing his hat high in the air. "Just watch me! I wouldn't miss a feed for anything."

Mother indulgently handed him a fresh cookie as he went out.

"You're the bestest ever!" he exclaimed.

Another minute brought twelve-year-old blue-eyed Grace to the door.

"Mother dear, I can't find baby's best dress. I have her all fluffed up except that. May I dress now?"

"Yes, dearie. I'll finish baby myself."

And so when Venna arrived, everyone, spic and span, was ready to meet her.

When Venna first entered the large living room in the Maddon home, it seemed to her that children popped out of every corner.

Mrs. Maddon proudly introduced each one, even holding out baby Ann for inspection.

"And this is our smallest, teeniest one," she said, as Venna took the bundle of lace.

"You little angel," said Venna, smiling. "I've been loving another baby Ann this summer." Then Venna told of the child's sickness and recovery.

"Brother Hallock is a man of great faith," said Sister Maddon. "I know him well. We'll be glad to get him back."

When they were all seated at the table, every little head bowed with their mother's.

"I think Grace may ask the blessing," said Sister Maddon.

"God bless the food prepared for our use. May it strengthen and help us for the work before us. Amen," said Grace softly.

Venna looked from one face to the other with admiration.

"What a perfect home picture, Sister Maddon! And this custom of asking the blessing—I like it so much. Something you seldom see in the East."

After a "homey" lunch, which Venna enjoyed more because of the merry faces of the children, Mrs. Maddon and Venna went upstairs alone.

"I want to show you some pictures of the West," she said, taking out a large portfolio full of photographs.

"This was my home," she said, looking fondly at a picture of a large, comfortable house with surrounding porches, upon which played the children.

"Bless their hearts! How they did love the freedom out there. There's no open places for them to play here."

"Are all Mormon families as large as yours?" asked Venna.

"Most of them are larger," returned Sister Maddon, laughing.

"How do you *ever* manage?" asked Venna in wondering admiration.

"That's what all the Eastern women say! My dear Mrs. Hadly, women in the East don't know how to really enjoy life. They *think* they do. They imagine that 'dolling up,' going to balls and theatres and whist parties, give them a good time. But they're not as happy as we are. They pity us and—we pity them!"

"No, I don't believe they know true happiness. One or two children is the limit as a rule—except among the lower classes."

"The lower classes then are the best off."

"But suppose, Sister Maddon, a husband turns out badly. Then a woman must have a struggle to get along."

"That happens sometimes," returned Mrs. Maddon. "But as a rule our men are as near perfect husbands as the Lord ever intended. You see our boys are brought up to be chaste and pure. There is an equal standard of morality for our boys and girls, so they don't sow their wild oats before they're married and then offer their wife a remnant of manhood. We Mormon women can't understand how some Eastern women marry these worn-out sports. I wouldn't want one for the father of my children. My darlings are my whole ambition in life. I believe I was created for that ambition and its attainment."

"Don't any of your girls ever long for a career?" asked Venna.

"Oh, yes, many of them. And Mormon parents always try to develop every talent a girl has. But even our ambitious women finally marry and have large families. They have to be in the world a few years to realize that the highest womanly ambition is to be a mother."

There was a general shouting among the children downstairs.

"Something is pleasing them," said Mother Maddon, laughing.

In a few minutes Teddy bounced in.

"What d'you think, mother? Brother Hallock's come back!" he declared excitedly.

"Already? Why, that's fine, to be sure. We'll come down directly."

"You bet it's dandy!" agreed Teddy, bouncing out again and going downstairs two steps at the time.

Mother Maddon turned to Venna.

"How those children do adore him! You see he lives with us when in the city and every spare minute he spends with those children—he certainly deserves a good, wholesome wife. But I don't have to worry about him yet. He has another year of mission work, and missionaries aren't allowed to speak of love to any woman. So I have a whole year to give him good advice!" she said, laughing. "Come, we must go down to him."

Venna needed no urging. She was anxious to talk with him.

Brother Hallock received both women with great friendliness. The children, fearful of letting him go, clung around him as he held out both hands.

There was great sympathy in the keen glance he gave Venna. He realized her state of mind by the great change in her.

"A little while with these youngsters would bring the roses back to your cheeks, Mrs. Hadly," he said, kindly.

"I'm sure it would," returned Venna, looking at the children with a wistful smile. "How fortunate this woman is!" she thought.

He noticed her expression.

"What do you think of a 'Mormon' family?" he asked.

"I think it is Theodore Roosevelt's idea of what every American family should be," returned Venna.

After a very happy afternoon and a promise to come again, Venna took her leave. Brother Hallock escorted her home.

"Won't you come in?" asked Venna when they reached the house.

"Not to-night, thank you. But if you are willing, I will call to-morrow afternoon."

And so they parted. Venna to a good night of refreshing sleep. Brother Hallock to a rather restless night, with dreams of his saving Venna from all kinds of catastrophes.

The next afternoon Venna lost herself in more discussion and explanation of the "Mormon" faith. Her afternoon in Brother Hallock's company would have been perfect, but for the fact that her Aunt Emily came in upon them unexpectedly. Venna introduced her to Brother Hallock. She frigidly acknowledged the introduction, said a few parting words to Venna—she was going away for two weeks with Dr. Hansom—and then quickly left the house.

Brother Hallock relieved Venna's embarrassment.

"Don't feel badly on my account," he said, smiling. "There are very few ministers' wives that tolerate us at all. We expect that."

The next morning's mail brought a short letter to Venna.

"Dear Venna:

"Dr. Hansom and I are grieved beyond words. Are you so under the spell of those evil-minded Mormons that you intend to disgrace us all? Do you stop for a moment to consider that all your friends will cast you off? Dr. Hansom said, 'I wouldn't want to acknowledge a Mormon as a relative.' But he is so good and kind he would not cast you off, for my sake. O, Venna, recover yourself, before it is too late and your life is ruined! Dr. Hansom will ask all his people to pray for your deliverance. I gave him your message, asking him to discuss the subject with you. He says, "There is nothing to discuss. As soon waste time talking over fairy tales."

"So you see his great and generous mind has only pity for you, dear. When we come back, let us come to the dear old Venna we always loved, with her simple faith.

"Yours always lovingly,
"Aunt Emily."

Venna laid the letter down with a sigh. Then she opened another from Ashfield.

"Dear Venna,

"This is just a short note from your Anna. How we all miss you more and more! I can't return to the city until the paralysis epidemic is over, so you have the advantage over me. I suppose by the time we come back you'll know all the good Mormons in the city.

"Mr. Soffy called and asked for your address. I told him you left word that I should give it to no one. He got very red and walked out with a very angry expression. Bud also wanted to write, so I held his hand and helped spell his words. Here is his letter enclosed. Let me know how you are and if you are overcoming your great sorrow. Time will show you, dear, it was all for the best.

"Lovingly,
"Anna."

Venna smiled as she unfolded Bud's letter.

"Dear Missus Hadly:

"Wot I can't spell, yer friend will. Ashfield is so powerful lonesome since yer went. They have it yer in Utah with the Mormons and thet yer husband has tin other wives. Yer friend says taint true, so don't yer think I believe it.

"Mr. Soffy give a sermon on Delusions—I got thet word right this time for I said it over an over all week. Every one said it was sure fine. Miss Mary said it was meant ter hit yer, an I up an' told her, Mr. Soffy was dirty mean ter cast inflections on yer. Miss Mary told *ma* wot I said, and she up an gave me a lickin. But wen I wus sore all over, I felt a sort o satisfactory in suffrin fer won I love. I up an tole Boss Holden this, an' he says yer worth all the humiliation we can give yer.

"Write ter me to yer friend so ma won't see it.

"Yours always in emotion,
"Bud."

"Dear Bud!" said Venna softly, "some day your devotion shall be repaid!"

CHAPTER XVI.

"For all eternity."

The winter of 1916-17 will always be a memorable one in America. The awful reports of the war in the Old World filled the New World with constant fear that we, too, would be dragged into it in spite of all overtures for Peace by President Wilson.

This public interest together with her activities in religious work brought Venna completely out of her solitude, and made her once more happy and ambitious. She opened her home to the young Mormon missionaries and never was there a time when two or three were not staying with her. So heartily did she embrace the Mormon faith, that it soon seemed as though it had always been hers, and her new friends seemed nearer to her than the old ones. Most of her society friends dropped her entirely, but Venna had no time for them now, so she did not miss their attention.

It hurt Venna to see her aunt's continual attitude of despair for her lost condition. She and Dr. Hansom were still Venna's friends, but their relations were strained and they seldom stayed long in one another's company. All Venna's efforts to discuss with them failed.

Summer came again, but Venna entertained no thoughts of the country. Both her time and her money were too much needed in the city. She had become quite expert in Red Cross work and enjoyed it more than anything else.

It was one week after America had declared war. Venna was reading the papers with intense interest when Brother Hallock called.

She had come to look for his frequent calls as a necessity. At last love had come into her life and Brother Hallock was her greatest joy. Together they constantly planned for the Church and Red Cross work.

"So it has come at last!" said Venna seriously.

"Yes, at last! America has tried to keep out of it; but we, too, must bear our share of the world's burden. I intend to do my part. Venna, I have news for you. I'm released."

"From what?"

"From my mission. I can go back West anytime now."

"You will go West?" she asked with a sudden fear of losing him.

"Very soon, yes; I feel as though I don't want to waste time. I'm going home to work off some of the debt incurred by my mission and then I shall volunteer."

Both stood silent for a few moments, looking into one another's eyes with a realization of a future of sacrifice.

"How can I possibly spare you?" she asked, laying her hand gently upon his arm.

Her touch thrilled him.

"Don't you think it will be hard for me?" he said, with emotion.

She stood thoughtful for a moment. She felt his great love for her, but then it was not permitted for him to speak of it. She would not tempt him to break mission rules.

She looked up smiling.

"When do you expect to go?"

"Next week," he answered, smiling his appreciation of her effort.

"You will write to me, of course?"

"Directly I arrive!" came promptly. "And you?"

"I won't tell you now what I intend doing. You might not approve," she replied, laughing.

"What new idea now?" he asked, looking curiously at her flushed, eager countenance.

"You must not know until you volunteer. So let me know when you go to France, won't you?"

So Brother Hallock left for the West the following week, wondering what surprise Venna had planned.

Everything seemed changed to Venna, after his departure.

The cold indifference of her society friends seemed to turn into a constant stinging rebuke. Many of her Mormon associates were only visitors in the East for the winter. She had grown fond of them all, and as one by one left for the West, she longed to go, too. Walter wrote as he had promised, but his letter was so disappointing, it was almost impossible for her to be her own smiling self.

How she had longed for that first letter! How she had watched the mails! Surely when he had returned home and had been honorably released, he would write of his love for her! These were her expectations, her longings.

Was it all a mistake after all? Had she only *imagined* he loved her?

This was the first letter from the man she loved—a kind, friendly letter, which her trembling hands had opened to her own chagrin.

"Salt Lake City.

"Dear Sister Venna:

"I meant to write to you sooner, but have been rushed here and there on business and social calls at such a rate, I have scarcely had time to eat. My dear sister, you can't conceive how strange an experience it is to come home from a mission. Everyone makes a great deal more of you than you deserve and mothers—well, if every mother acted like my mother did (I expect they all do), the boys must all feel fine about their small sacrifices. Mother follows me from room to room, and whenever I'm at home she tries her best to make me realize I'm just the grandest son in Christendom, so do my sisters. The girls and mother vie with one another to excel in their goodness to me. If I were not well dosed with the scorn and abuse of the East, I'm afraid this wonderful home adoration would unbalance me, and deprive me of my humility.

"It seems mighty good to be in dear old Salt Lake again; but it is so strange, Venna, how all my former companions seem changed to me. Of course, I know it is I who have changed the most. I have grown away from them in many ways. I find myself criticising many little things in their lives that I never noticed before I left for the East. I find myself correcting them, and they laughingly tell me I have gotten the 'preaching habit' and must come down to earth a little.

"Yes, there's no doubt a missionary's life takes one beyond himself, as it were. I wish all the boys had the privilege of living in the mission field for two years. I believe every one of them would lose the desire for small follies.

"Give my love to all the saints and especially to dear Sister Maddon.

"Write to me soon and tell me all the 'doings' of the Mission. God bless you in your wonderful devotion.

"Your brother in the Gospel,

"Walter Hallock."

"What a cool, ordinary letter!" thought Venna as she re-read his letter for the twentieth time.

She was dressing to go out for a ride with Mrs. Maddon who had phoned to her in the morning asking her to take a few hours from her duties to ride out into the country, and "we will have a good old chat," she had added.

Dear Mrs. Maddon! How Venna loved this cheerful friend. In spite of herself, Venna always brightened in her company. Yes, an afternoon with her would be refreshing.

As the bell announced her coming Venna quickly folded Walter's letter and tucked it away in her waist. In true womanly fashion, she carried that first letter always with her.

Soon the two women were comfortably settled and whizzing through the hot city streets to the cool, green country without. Venna was at the wheel. She seldom had a chauffeur now, much to the disgust of her aunt and Dr. Hansom. She tried to explain that she wished to be in good practice—some day she would drive in France—but this was listened to with a smile.

Once out on almost deserted country roads, Venna slackened speed, and the two friends gazed out upon the passing panorama of sunlit fields and dark, cool woodlands with evident satisfaction.

"How I envy Anna Halloway!" exclaimed Venna suddenly. "Did you know I received a letter from her lately? As soon as they reached the West, they looked around for real country life high up in the mountains. You know both Anna and her husband hate city life. They found a place called 'Ephraim,' and they've bought a home there. Anna says she looks at the mountains and feels nearer heaven already. She's so happy to have such a place to bring up her babe in. I'm glad for her, but I miss her so!"

"Is she the only one you miss?" asked Sister Maddon, laughing. "And is she the only one you have heard from lately?"

Venna blushed and gave the machine a little spurt.

"Oh, no," she returned, trying to look indifferent. "I meant to tell you I heard from Walter about a week ago. He wishes me to give you his love. Here is his letter. Won't you read it?"

Sister Maddon read and then handed the letter back to Venna.

"Good as no letter at all—don't you think so?" she questioned Venna, smiling.

The machine received another spurt, as Venna determined to conceal her hurt.

"Why, no," she answered calmly, "it was very kind of him to write at all when he is so busy."

Mrs. Maddon laughed one of her joyous little ripples.

"Now, look here, Venna dear, I didn't persuade you to come out to-day just because your health needed it. It isn't only much needed fresh air that has paled you lately. You mustn't mind a mother like me getting interested in your great love for Walter, and his great love for you. You don't mind me speaking frankly, dear?"

Venna turned to her friend impulsively.

"I couldn't mind anything from *you*, Sister Maddon, but you've guessed wrong this time. That letter ought to prove it to you."

"It proves nothing—except that Walter won't propose to a rich girl when he is without a cent and must soon go to war."

"How do you know *that*?" exclaimed Venna, her large eyes scanning her friend's face eagerly.

"Because he told me so!" came with another joyous ripple.

"You don't mean"—

"Yes, I *do* mean that your place is out West as soon as you can get there. We'll miss you here, but your place is with that good boy of ours as long as he is here. Don't lose time. He may be in France soon. *He'll* never propose to you, you'll have to show him how!"

Venna brought the car to a sudden standstill. The road was empty. She buried her face on Mother Maddon's shoulder and sobbed for joy. The mother's heart was touched.

"Tears of joy, aren't they, dear?" she said, patting the curls lovingly. "Just think how *he* feels, away out West. We mustn't lose any time."

———

Two weeks later Venna and Walter stood smiling into one another's eyes with the rapture of a great love.

Suddenly Walter's eyes clouded. "Even if I had not volunteered, Venna, I would have nothing to offer you until I had proved myself, but this war— God knows when it will end, and then every man has to start life again, perhaps blind or crippled."

As he spoke, Venna trembled with a fearful premonition of the world's future sorrows, but when he finished, she looked her love into his soul, smiling bravely.

"How better can a woman show her love than when a man needs her most? You know a Mormon girl marries for eternity, not just for the few years of this life—and if you come back from the war afflicted, who could better care for you than I? As for money, I've been thinking a great deal about my wealth to-day. It seems wicked to be rich, when so many are starving. I shall keep a very little for the future. The rest of my wealth I'll give to the Belgians and French. So you see, Walter, neither of us will have money after the war. With so great a love in our hearts, should we think of material things?"

"I have determined to go to France also, Walter," she added, smiling.

"*You* go to France?" he asked, surprised.

"And why not? Should I not be as patriotic as you? Women are needed badly. I am quite a Red Cross nurse now, you know."

"Yes, you're right," he answered seriously. "But I had never thought of *you* going. What a world of sacrifice we are now living in!"

"Let us try to hold our heads high and smile at adversity," she replied, smiling back at him.

"For God and America!" he added, taking her tenderly in his arms. "O Venna," he said, passionately, "what have I done to deserve such a woman as you! For all eternity! How little the outside world realizes the inspiration of that word. Shall we go through the temple together, Venna? Shall we be married there before we go to Europe?"

"Yes, Walter—for all eternity!" she answered softly.

CHAPTER XVII.

Everywhere Ruin, standing side by side with the Sign of the Cross!

In the little town of Behericourt, a few miles from Noyon, France, a young Red Cross nurse alighted from her machine, and took a general survey of the ruined homes. Her mind had become accustomed to thinking of disaster and ruin, for everywhere the same sad spectacle met her pitying eyes, but her heart throbbed anew with every fresh scene. Here were about seventy-five helpless souls, living in their ruined homes, needing all of life's necessities.

She did not gaze long. She stepped up to the nearest house and knocked on the broken door.

A little child of ten, with pale, drawn face, and large fear-stricken eyes, cautiously opened the door.

"I'm a friend, little one," said Venna, smiling.

The child recognized the Red Cross and nodded her head vigorously.

"Come in," she said excitedly, and then vanished to carry the good news to others.

Venna entered the kitchen. In it were four broken chairs, a broken table and a broken stove. On some nails in the walls were hung broken kitchen utensils.

"It was the German idea to break everything from the greatest to the least," thought Venna sadly. "What homes for these poor people to return to!"

An old man of seventy and a woman not much younger entered with the little girl. There was no smile of welcome on either face—they had forgotten how to smile, but their eyes looked eagerly questioning.

"Have you brought us news, madam—news—tell us—what about them?" the old man asked excitedly.

Venna's eyes saddened. After all, her great wealth couldn't buy the most important things in France!

"Now, my dear, good people, I have no news today. I have come to see what you most need and to try to help you."

The old folks looked disappointedly at one another and then the old woman turned to Venna in tears.

"Give us news of our children and we can get along."

"Come, my good people, let us sit down here somehow, and talk things over. Tell me all about your children—maybe I can find out something."

They managed to prop the chairs and sit down, the little girl clinging close to Venna as the one bright spot in the dingy home.

"How many have you away? Just where are they?" asked Venna.

"God knows where they are!" exclaimed the old man, trembling. "There were two other girls, sixteen and eighteen, and their father and mother—all of us happy and working hard to keep together. The father and the two girls were compelled by the Germans to report at the Chateau—they took them to Germany to work—God, what will they do with my girls?" Here the old man moaned piteously.

"The mother died since of a broken heart," said the old woman, continuing the story her husband was not able to finish. "Would to God they were all dead! We'll soon go, too. Who'll take her?" she asked, pointing to the frightened child.

Venna patted the child's head.

"She'll be well taken care of—by the Red Cross."

"Will she?" asked the old woman eagerly. "That's a piece of comfort to know."

Venna felt she was lingering too long.

"I must be back to Noyon at a stated time, so I must not stay as long as I would like to," she said. "Come, tell me some things you need. You surely need something?"

"Everything," replied the woman hopelessly. "We need windows—it's so cold—every one is broken."

Venna's heart ached. Even her money could not buy *glass* here!

"We can't get glass," she said, "but I'll come with help in a day or two, and we'll try to bring something that will keep the cold out."

"Then where can we get the light?"

"I really don't know," said Venna as cheerfully as she could, "but I'll talk it over at headquarters. Good-bye for a few days. Take courage. We'll do our very best for you."

As Venna left the house, and went to the next, the child stood watching her go with eyes full of longing for the promised future.

When Venna had finished her rounds, her heart was unusually heavy. She could not get hardened to these scenes of misery. What an experience had been hers! New York and its associations seemed in another world of the remote past.

Her husband's letters had come frequently and been a great source of courage. But for the last month she could get no news from him. Evidently his letters were lost—or—she dared not think anything worse—surely if anything had happened to him, she would have been notified, yet—the cruel doubt made her shudder, and to-day, as she drove toward Noyon, she felt a deep sympathy for those she had just left—the poor, helpless people clamoring for news. News! How she longed for news herself!

As she approached the top of a hill, a sign came in full view.

"Cette pointe est vue de Tenmeni. N'arrettez pas"—(This point is in sight of the enemy. Do not stop.)

Venna gave a shudder as she passed by quickly.

On the other side of the hill she beheld the ruins of the great castle of Coucy. The Lords of Coucy had been the proudest in the surrounding country. They held themselves superior to kings. Now this massive castle was a heap of dust-colored stone.

"Surely God is no respecter of persons," thought Venna.

When she reached Noyon and turned in at the Evacuating Hospital, she was greeted with a laugh from one of the nurses.

"You are just in time!" she said. "Fifty pink and blue pajamas have just come for the men. They'll surely scrap over them if *you* don't give them out. There are not enough to go around."

Venna smiled.

"I'll take them in and have them draw lots," she said.

As Venna entered the convalescing tent, there was a general delighted murmur of welcome. That she was the idol of the soldiers was plainly seen by the expressions on their rugged faces.

She held up one pink pajama and one blue.

"Now, boys," she said, smiling brightly, "there are just twenty-five of each. I wish we had enough for all, but we have not. What do you say if we draw lots?"

"Good!" came unanimously as each soldier eyed the alluring garments with envy.

The first to draw a pink pajama was the "baby of the ward," a boy of eighteen who was stretched out with a fractured hip. He was so delighted with his new present that he begged to have it put on immediately.

"Le Bebe' Rose!" shouted the soldiers.

That night the soldiers in their new pajamas were carried joyously into the concert tent, the envy of all those who were less fortunate in drawing lots.

Venna looked on with a smile on her face and sadness in her heart.

"After all, these brave men are boys at heart!"

Later on in the evening, when the moon was full up, Venna walked out alone. She felt that she must calm her perturbed thoughts.

Where was her husband? Her anxiety was getting beyond her endurance.

For ten minutes she walked and prayed.

Suddenly, like a huge beetle, a boche airplane swooped low over Noyon! Then came an awful crash!

Venna stood fascinated, gazing up at this awful bird of destruction. The search-lights were in full play. Venna could plainly see the cross on the under side of the wings. What a hideous mockery!

A soldier sprang to Venna's side.

"Madam! The shrapnel! Come back against this house!"

But the warning was too late. Another bomb fell. A piece of flying shrapnel struck Venna.

Her hands clasped in prayer and her lips moved inaudibly as she sank upon the ground.

Tenderly the soldier leaned over Venna's still form. The moonlight lit the ghastly wound in her forehead.

"Dead!" exclaimed the soldier, horrified.

Gently he lifted Venna in his big, strong arms and made for the hospital.

"Damn!" he muttered. "Why didn't the hellish thing hit me?"

CHAPTER XVIII.

"Somewhere in France."

In a convalescing tent sat a young officer, writing. When finished, he took up the letter for perusal.

"Venna Dearest:

"You have doubtless worried at my long silence.

"A month ago I was brought here from the front, seriously wounded. When I finally came to myself, I feared worrying you, so did not let you know until all danger was past. I prayed to live to go again to the front, and God granted my prayer.

"O Venna, my brave little wife! How I long to clasp you again in my arms! But we are many miles apart. God grant that this cruel war will soon be over, and that you and I may meet again in dear old, free America.

"In one week I shall go to the front again.

"The doctors cannot understand my miraculous recovery, but you and I, dear, know what faith can do. Pray for me always.

"Your devoted husband,

"Walter."

While he was folding the letter in an envelope, a private entered.

"A message for you, Capt. Hallock," he said, saluting his superior.

Capt. Hallock took the message and read.

He turned pale and grasped the chair convulsively.

When left alone, he covered his face with his hands and sobbed.

"My Venna killed! God! How can I stand it!" he cried in agony of spirit.

He felt a hand laid upon his shoulder. With quick self-control he turned and looked up into the face of one of his comrades.

"Bad news, Hallock?"

"My wife is dead!" returned Hallock with a stern compression of his lips.

There was silence for a moment while his comrade looked his sympathy into his friend's eyes. Then he held out his soldier's hand which Hallock grasped.

"Remember, Hallock," he said with emotion, "when you converted me to your Mormon faith, you comforted me with the thought that my dead wife had simply passed on before. There is no death. We will both have our loved ones soon—probably *very* soon, for next week comes the German drive with you and I at the front!"

Hallock straightened himself up bravely.

"As God wills!" he calmly returned.

—

The battle was finished. On the field lay the wounded and dying. The night was fast closing in to add its darkness to the horror and the gloom of it all.

Most of the prostrate forms were quiet in death, but many were moaning piteously.

"Is there no help near?" asked one of them. "Water! Oh, for a drink!"

Hallock felt for his flask. It was empty.

"No," returned Hallock. "No help yet."

"Comrades," he cried, raising his voice as high as his feeble condition would allow—"we are all soon to go to that other shore from which no man returns. Let us go gladly, heroically—like soldiers, not like cowards caught in the jaws of death. Remember! We are entering a glorious life!"

With the last words he fell back and the blackness of night settled over the battlefield.

A bright shaft of light suddenly shone high above Hallock's head. It drew nearer and nearer, until it dazzled him with its brilliancy.

With a thrill of unearthly joy Hallock beheld, approaching through the wondrous light, Venna! His glorified Venna!

His arms outstretched in welcome.

"I have come to take you over," she said, softly, as she encircled her arms about him.

"For all eternity!" he murmured happily.

CONCLUSION.

On the shores of Eternity, Venna and Walter communed together.

"At Last!" said Walter joyously. "How wonderful our life is here!"

"And to think that greater glory will yet be ours as we eternally progress!" exclaimed Venna in ecstasy.

"Is it not strange," returned Walter, "that our earthly troubles seem as though they had never been!"

"Ah! dear heart! If the world could only see beyond the veil!"

At this moment she looked along the shore with sudden joy.

"Here comes Daddy!" she said as a holy joy suffused her radiant countenance.

Beside him walked a beautiful woman.

"It is your mother, Venna!" said Walter.

Venna pressed her cheek fondly against Walter's.

"If this is Paradise," she whispered, "I dare not think of Heaven!"

Milton Keynes UK
Ingram Content Group UK Ltd.
UKHW030838021124
450589UK00006B/690